# 100 PLANTS TO FEED THE MONARCH

Create a Healthy Habitat to Sustain North America's Most Beloved Butterfly

THE XERCES SOCIETY

Eric Lee-Mäder, Stephanie Frischie, Emma Pelton,
Sarina Jepsen, Stephanie McKnight, and Scott Hoffman Black

Storey Publishing

**The mission of Storey Publishing is to serve our customers by publishing practical information that encourages personal independence in harmony with the environment.**

Edited by Deborah Burns
Art direction and book design by Michaela Jebb
Text production by Erin Dawson

Cover photography by Front: © herreid/iStock.com, top; Row 1 l. to r. © Dembinsky Photo Associates/Alamy Stock Photo, © watcher fox/Shutterstock.com, © B. Christopher/Alamy Stock Photo, © Andrew Greaves/Alamy Stock Photo, © Botanic World/Alamy Stock Photo, © Florapix/Alamy Stock Photo, © vodolej/stock.adobe.com, © John Sullivan/Alamy Stock Photo, © Krystyna Szulecka/Alamy Stock Photo, © ANGHI/iStock.com; Row 2 l. to r. © NNehring/iStock.com, © Zoonar GmbH/Alamy Stock Photo, © ArtofNatureandLight/stock.adobe.com, © Skip Moody/Dembinsky Photo Associates/Alamy/Alamy Stock Photo, © Ivan Smuk/Shutterstock.com, © timmy/iStock.com, © Kyle Selcer/Alamy Stock Photo, © Nadezhda_Nesterova/iStock.com, © Tamara Harding/stock.adobe.com, © Christopher Price/Alamy Stock Photo; Row 3 l. to r. © dutchlight/stock.adobe.com, © mashimara/iStock.com, © helga_sm/stock.adobe.com, © Belikart/iStock.com, © Keir Morse, © sbonk/iStock.com, © WILDLIFE GmbH/Alamy Stock Photo, © Khatawut Chaemchamras/Alamy Stock Photo, © Panther Media GmbH/Alamy Stock Photo, © ekim/stock.adobe.com; Row 4 l. to r. © Shawn Fair/iStock.com, © ivanastar/iStock.com, © QwazzMe Photo/iStock.com, © Rafail/stock.adobe.com, © Kevin Schafer/Alamy Stock Photo, © Bill Brooks/Alamy Stock Photo, © linjerry/stock.adobe.com, © Hanna Tor/Alamy Stock Photo, © Steffen Hauser/botanikfoto/Alamy Stock Photo, © ariadna126/stock.adobe.com; Row 5 l. to r. © desertsolitaire/iStock.com, © NNehring/iStock.com, © TYNZA/iStock.com, © James Mundy, Nature's Ark Photography/Alamy Stock Photo, © Andyworks/iStock.com, © Kevin Knight/Alamy Stock Photo, © Zigmunds Kluss/stock.adobe.com, © agenturfotografin/stock.adobe.com, © NNehring/iStock.com, © na9179126124/stock.adobe.com; Back: © Lauren Hedien/Getty Images, left; © helga_sm/stock.adobe.com, right; Spine: © Martin Ruegner/Getty Images

Interior photography credits appear on page 288.
Illustrations by © A. James Gustafson
Maps by Ilona Sherratt © Storey Publishing, based on information supplied by The Xerces Society



Storey Publishing
210 MASS MoCA Way
North Adams, MA 01247
storey.com

Printed in China through World Print
10 9 8 7 6 5 4 3 2 1

Library of Congress Cataloging-in-Publication Data on file

# Contents

# PREFACE

Growing up in Nebraska, I was fortunate to live in an area where monarchs showed up every spring and came back through on their way south every fall. They were among the biggest and most noticeable butterflies. As a kid, I loved to watch them flutter through, looking for milkweed or mates, or on their long migration to overwintering sites in Mexico. In a single day we sometimes saw thousands of monarchs fly past on their journey south.

If you grew up almost anywhere in the continental United States or southern Canada, you are probably familiar with these fascinating animals. Graceful and beautiful, monarchs stand out due to their large size and vivid orange-and-black coloring. They are often the only butterfly people can identify.

This book is designed to help you help the monarch butterfly. Look through the pages and see which milkweed host plants and which nectar plants are native in your area. Then pick the ones that will fit best in your space, plant and water them—and you will have created a habitat for monarchs.

Of course, do not use pesticides, especially insecticides, as these kill monarchs and other beneficial insects. And make sure you tell your neighbors what you are doing and why—we need as many people as possible to take action. We are always heartened to hear the stories of entire neighborhoods getting involved; this truly gives us hope.

There is one last very important step. Sit in a comfortable chair with a favorite drink, enjoy your flower-filled landscape, and watch the monarchs and other butterflies add color to your life. You can feel excited to be part of the solution, saving the monarchs so they will be with us for years to come.

— **Scott Hoffman Black,** Executive Director, The Xerces Society

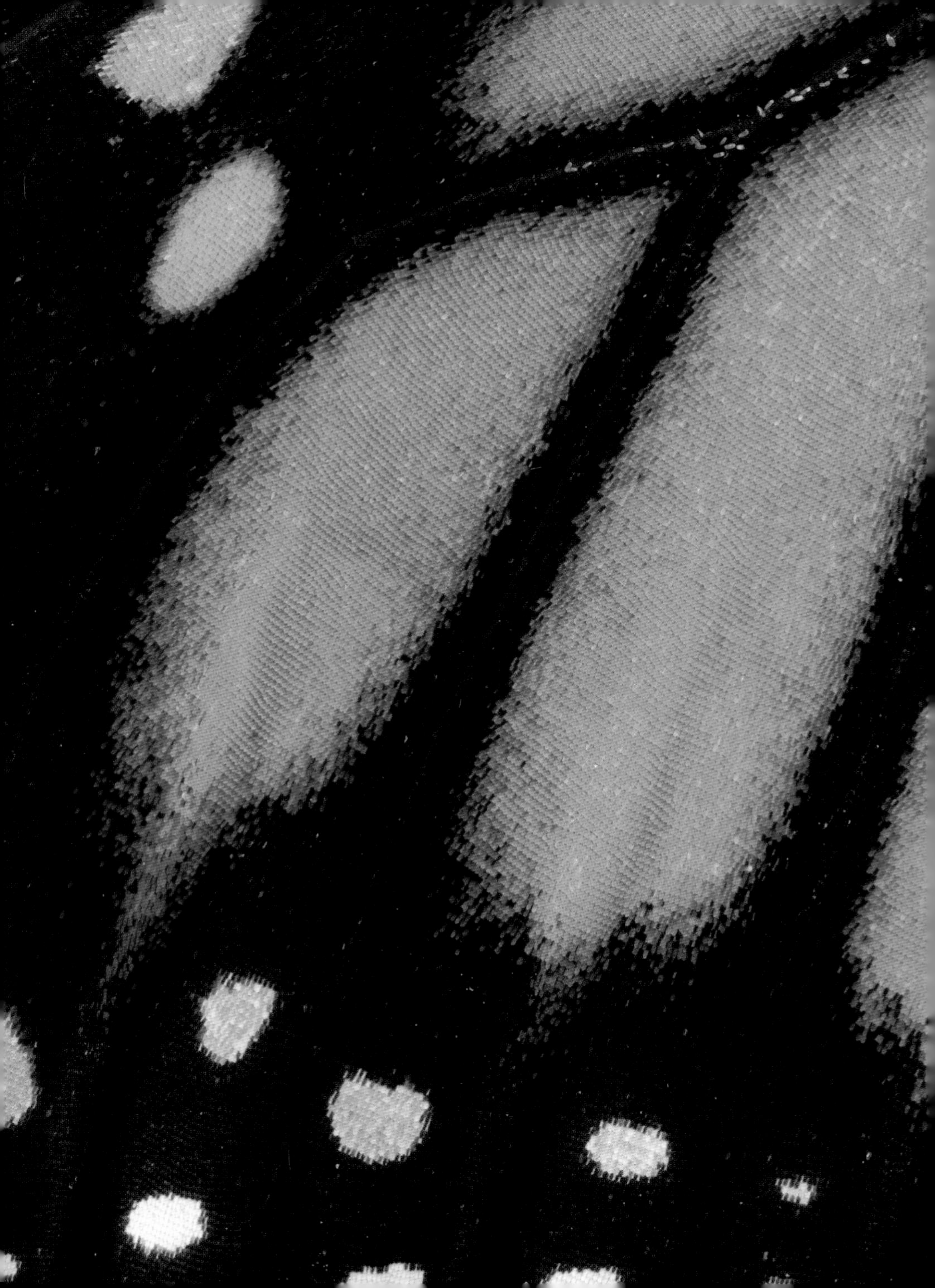

PART I

# North American Royalty

One of the remarkable things about the monarch butterfly (*Danaus plexippus*) is that although it is a single species, it largely exists as two separate populations: one east of the Rocky Mountains, and one to the west. Individuals may periodically cross this Great Divide, but the majority of monarchs belong to distinct but equally epic dynasties, generations of mass-migrating relatives.

Smaller scattered populations of this species also exist elsewhere, yet the majority of monarchs on Earth occur within these two famous migrating populations. Both have compelling stories of persistence and resilience, and both face increasing challenges.

Ranging from the Great Plains and southern prairie provinces to the Atlantic coast, Eastern monarchs are renowned for migrating incredibly long distances to their overwintering sites in the oyamel fir ("sacred fir") forests in the mountains west of Mexico City. In fact, during the fall migration, many monarchs fly more than 3,000 miles (some fly up to 4,000 miles!) to arrive among millions of others, seeking shelter in the mountain forest canopy from harsh weather.

The oyamel forest sites provide the perfect microclimate for monarchs: not so cold that the butterflies freeze and not so warm that they become active and burn too many calories, expending energy they will need for the trip north. This precise climate is vital, because the same monarch that migrated south will return as far north as Texas in the spring, seeking places to lay eggs.

Astonishingly, the animal making this journey weighs less than a penny. Imagine attempting this arduous trip, buffeted by thunderstorms, navigating vast stretches where the landscapes may be monocultures of corn or soybean or green lawn or concrete, looking for flowers to fuel your flight across the continent. It is truly an amazing feat.

Western monarchs make a slightly shorter but equally remarkable journey—one that traverses some of the most challenging landscapes in North America, including deserts, mountain ranges, and enormous agricultural lands virtually devoid of habitat.

Overwintering in small forested areas along the Pacific coast, from just north of San Francisco south to Baja, Western monarchs migrate inland to breed. Over the course of the migration season they travel across the West, floating above southwestern deserts, the Great Basin, the inland Northwest, and as far north as southern British Columbia.

Although the western population is smaller than its eastern counterpart, monarchs in the West are a remarkable example of animal survival. Not only have they lost overwintering habitat along the California coast to development, but they also face the Central Valley, one of the most intensively farmed landscapes on Earth, where pesticide use is widespread. During their life they may migrate from some of the most urbanized places on the West Coast to remote wild lands where few humans exist. Whether they can continue to survive this remarkable journey is a question increasingly asked.

Unfortunately, the days of seeing thousands of monarchs may be numbered. As we write this, the Eastern monarch numbers are down by two-thirds, a fraction of the hundreds of millions that migrated in the 1990s. Western monarchs are struggling even more, having declined by more than 99 percent in fewer than 40 years.

Monarchs can be saved, if we act. Their needs are actually quite simple:

- Milkweed plants on which to lay eggs, and where caterpillars feed and grow
- Nectar-rich flowers to sustain the adults as they reproduce and migrate over long distances
- Areas that are free of poisons such as insecticides

All can be provided in parks, along roadsides, on the edges of farms—and in your own yard. This last point is the purpose of this book. Although we need to protect what remains of larger natural areas, lots of small patches of habitat can help restore the greatness of the monarch migration. A simple patch of milkweeds and a couple of other wildflowers next to your own front door can be the place where a tiny egg hatches and grows to become part of an epic story.

# 1

# The Life of a Monarch

A monarch butterfly starts out as an egg on a leaf—typically in an open and sunny space, exposed to the sky and the universe beyond.

More specifically, a monarch's life begins with a milkweed plant.

Milkweeds are the sole food source for monarch caterpillars. In the process of consuming the plant, they absorb and retain part of its complex chemical ecology. You are what you eat, as they say, and monarchs are an extraordinary assemblage of milkweed chemistry that they carry throughout their life. Even as mature, free-flying adult butterflies, they frequently return to milkweed flowers as one of their preferred nectar plants. Perhaps it's a homecoming of sorts when they stop by for a drink.

We can support that homecoming by restoring more habitat for the beloved and beleaguered monarch. To maximize our impact, however, let's take a closer look at the biology of the world's most famous butterfly.

## A Shape-Shifting Life

A monarch egg is barely the size of a pinhead, or the tip of a pencil lead. If you find one, you'll notice its off-white or slightly yellow color. Upon very close inspection, you'll see lines of ridges running from top to bottom. This egg remains glued in place on a milkweed leaf for three to five days, depending on the temperature, until it hatches and the tiny pale caterpillar (usually less than two-tenths of an inch [5 mm] long) emerges into the world.

During the next several weeks, this small being will develop through four distinct life stages—egg, caterpillar, chrysalis, and adult. This type of development is known as **complete metamorphosis**.

Complete metamorphosis is different from **simple or incomplete metamorphosis**, in which an immature insect resembles a smaller version of its adult form. For example, grasshoppers, which undergo incomplete metamorphosis, hatch from eggs and look like tiny versions of their adult selves, periodically shedding their exoskeleton as they grow.

### Monarch Multiplication

One of the mysteries of monarch butterflies is their approach to courtship, which is less elaborate than that of other butterflies and moths. Unlike other butterflies, female monarchs cannot easily rebuff mates. Instead, the male monarch tackles a

## LIFE CYCLE OF A MONARCH

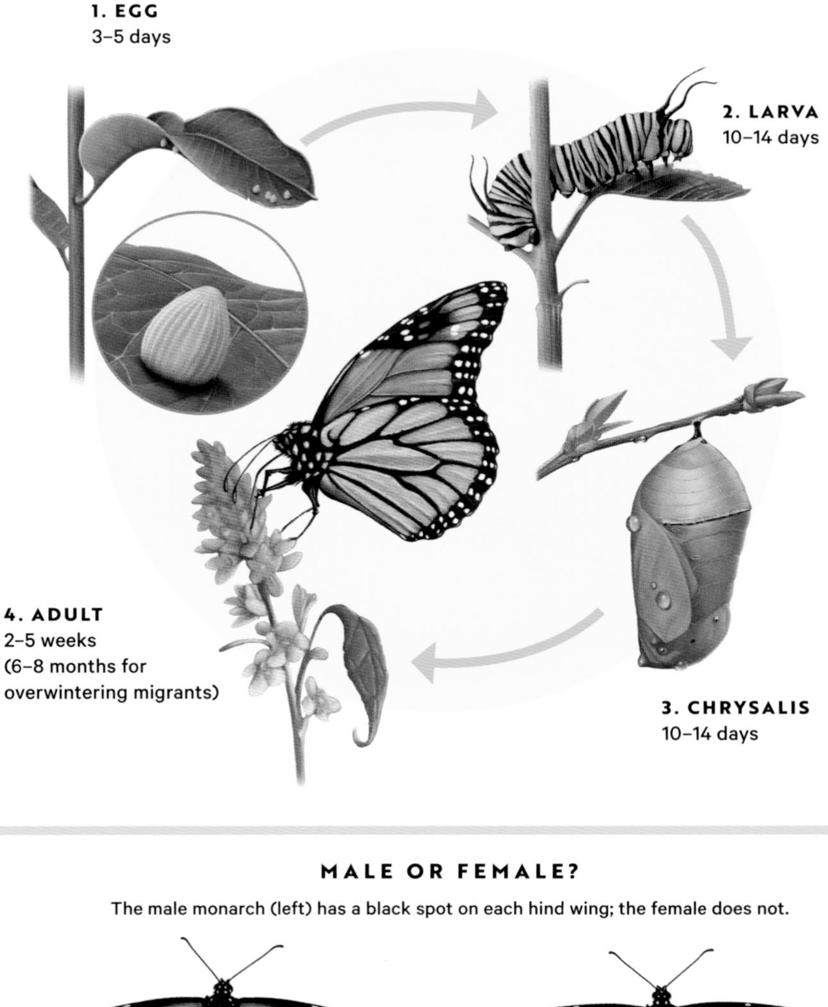

**1. EGG**
3–5 days

**2. LARVA**
10–14 days

**3. CHRYSALIS**
10–14 days

**4. ADULT**
2–5 weeks
(6–8 months for overwintering migrants)

### MALE OR FEMALE?

The male monarch (left) has a black spot on each hind wing; the female does not.

A monarch egg (left) is miniscule, ridged, and pearly white. Out of it hatches a tiny caterpillar that immediately begins munching the milkweed leaf on which it is born. Caterpillar droppings, called frass (arrow at right), are a clue that monarch caterpillars are or recently were on the plant.

female midflight, or grabs a resting female, and then attempts to couple with her in a struggle that can last for many minutes.

Karen Oberhauser, a prominent monarch researcher, and other scientists have been intrigued by the evolutionary origins of this mating behavior. They hypothesize that it is possibly related to the overwintering phase. At some point in the history of the species, older, worn-out males who were unlikely to survive the winter may have made a last-ditch attempt to reproduce. Once this behavior evolved, it became a mating strategy used in both overwintering and summer generations.

Successful mating can last up to 16 hours, during which time the male passes a sperm packet called a **spermatophore** to the tip of the female's abdomen, where it provides both sperm and a protein boost. The sperm then fertilize the eggs as they pass down the female's egg-laying tube. Monarchs can mate several times in their lives.

## The Egg

On average, a healthy monarch female will produce about 400 eggs in her lifetime. Whether she successfully lays many of these depends on how long she lives and the availability of milkweeds to deposit them on.

Milkweeds, mostly in the genus *Asclepias,* are the only plants that monarch caterpillars can feed on. Yet even when milkweeds are available, females are still selective about where they lay their eggs. With their chemically sensitive feet, monarchs "taste" a leaf and decide if it is a good spot to place an egg. If it is, they lay their eggs individually, generally one per leaf.

The females tend to avoid laying eggs on milkweeds that already have caterpillars feeding on them or that have older and tougher leaves. Instead, they seek out tender plants with less competition.

## Munching on Milkweeds

Monarch caterpillars spend most of their time eating. As a tiny hatchling, the soft-bodied caterpillar usually eats its own eggshell before starting in on the milkweed. In the days ahead it will consume a tremendous amount relative to its size and grow increasingly larger.

Like adult insects, caterpillars have an exoskeleton. Although they may look soft and squishy, their exoskeleton is actually a hardened structure that protects the inner organs and muscles but does not expand to accommodate growth. In order to grow larger, a caterpillar must shed its exoskeleton (**molt**).

In fact, a monarch caterpillar molts five times before forming a chrysalis. With each stage (**instar**) between molting, the front and back **protuberances** (the antennae-like appendages on its head and rump) also lengthen and can be used to identify the caterpillar's instar stage.

## Metamorphosis Begins with a "J"

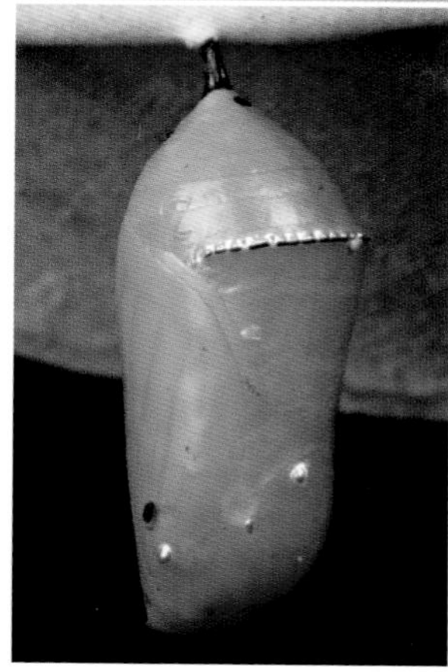

In its final molt, a monarch caterpillar transforms into a **chrysalis** or **pupa**, the mummylike stage between caterpillar and adult. Often it wanders away from the host milkweed plant, onto surrounding vegetation, nearby fences, or other structures, where it attaches itself in place with a silk pad.

As the transformation begins, the caterpillar hangs head-down in a "J" shape. It sheds its exoskeleton one last time to reveal a jade green casing, which quickly hardens into a protective shell.

## WHAT HAPPENS INSIDE A CHRYSALIS?

The science behind this seemingly magical transformation is complex and still not completely understood. It is regulated by a series of hormonal changes that result in an almost complete cellular rearrangement of the caterpillar's body, transforming it into an adult butterfly. If you were to watch the entire process, you would see it begin with the caterpillar hanging head-down—yet after metamorphosis the butterfly emerges with its head up. Head and tail thus change places entirely, over the course of just a week or two.

Amazingly, even with this significant rearrangement, monarchs carry the protective chemicals they acquire as caterpillars from milkweed all the way through into adulthood. Equally fascinating, some insects that undergo complete metamorphosis (the tobacco hawk moth is one) seem to retain behavior learned as caterpillars into adulthood, although whether this occurs with monarchs is still unknown.

The term ***chrysalis*** applies to both this developmental stage and the casing. It comes from the Greek word *khrusos* (meaning gold), referring to the reflective metallic coloration found on the pupae of many butterflies, including monarchs.

Just before the adult emerges (known as **eclosing**), the chrysalis usually changes color and then breaks open. The butterfly crawls out and pumps its compressed wings to fill them with a bloodlike fluid called **hemolymph**. Then, within moments, the monarch takes its first flight.

### Two Very Different Life Spans

Spring and summer monarchs typically survive only two to five weeks as adults. The overwintering generation, on the other hand, may live six to nine months—completing the fall migration to overwintering sites and dispersing back to breeding grounds the following spring. In total, at least four generations are produced over the spring and summer, with the last generation migrating to overwintering sites.

For spring and summer monarchs, roughly half of their life is spent as a caterpillar and half as an adult. Given this brief existence, the availability of milkweeds and nectar plants at the right time is fundamental to monarch survival.

#### MALE OR FEMALE?

You can tell the sex of a monarch by looking at the hind wings. Males have a distinctive black dot in the middle of the wing, which marks the location of a scent gland that produces pheromones intended to attract females. As well as lacking these glands, females have thicker black wing veins than males do. (See photos on page 13.)

## On the Wing

The native range of monarchs covers most of temperate North America, Central America, and northern South America. They have been introduced to Hawaii, other Pacific islands, Australia, New Zealand, Spain, and Portugal, where they feed on exotic milkweed species or milkweed relatives such as *Calotropis* spp. Yet monarchs are most numerous in North America, and it is only here that long-distance migration occurs.

Migration begins in the spring as overwintered monarchs take flight, radiating north from Mexico and inland from coastal California. With luck and good conditions, these females will find milkweeds and lay eggs before dying. The offspring of Eastern monarchs will continue northward, and the offspring of Western monarchs will move farther inland. This movement continues with each generation throughout the spring and summer.

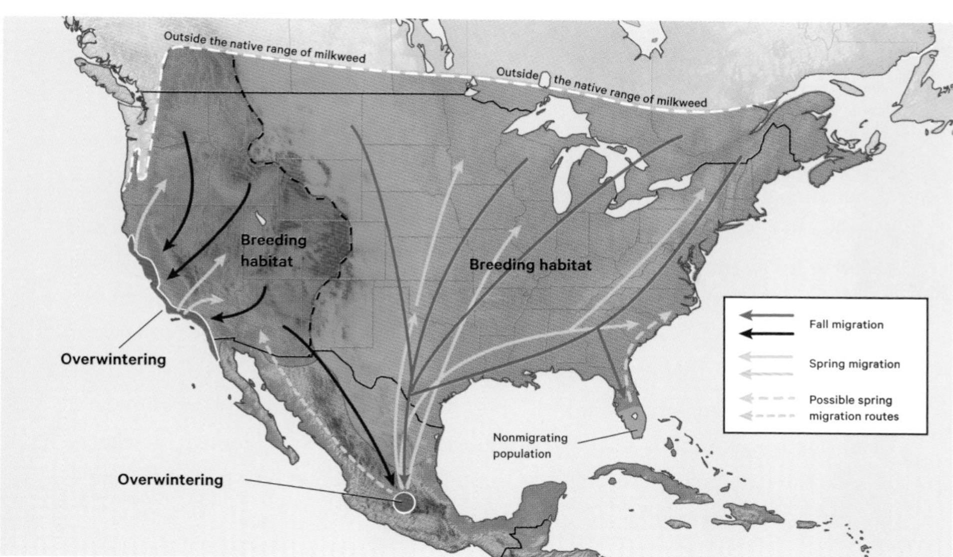


The fall and spring migration routes of the Western and Eastern monarch are separated by the Rocky Mountains.

As fall approaches, most milkweeds go dormant, and remaining monarchs start the journey toward the overwintering grounds. Migratory monarchs may sense Earth's magnetic fields, using an internal sun compass and possibly other signals to navigate back to the same overwintering sites—even the very same trees—that their ancestors inhabited the year before.

Although monarchs migrate individually, sometimes large numbers will pass through a given area, possibly due to weather conditions or local geography. Exceptionally large groups of migrating monarchs have even been detected by weather radar! Temporary clusters of migrating monarchs are also sometimes spotted in trees where they spend the night or take shelter from wind and storms. Known as **roosts**, such aggregations are most commonly seen in nectar- and water-rich areas near the Great Lakes, in the southern Great Plains, and in the Southwest.

Most monarchs follow the same migration pathways used by previous butterflies year after year, but the Eastern and Western monarch populations are not entirely separate. Studies have shown that some monarchs from the West (particularly the Southwest) migrate to central Mexico, where they overwinter alongside

Eastern monarchs, while others from the same area migrate to overwintering sites in California. What prompts this kind of migration shift remains unknown.

## Overwintering

When monarchs reach their overwintering grounds—typically September or October in California, and October or November in central Mexico—they cluster together for warmth, settling in for the winter. The majority of overwintering monarchs are in reproductive **diapause** (not mating or laying eggs), conserving fat for survival and spring dispersal. They are not completely inactive, however. On warm days in the winter, they may seek out nearby water or nectar.

Although the majority of North American monarchs migrate, warm climates (such as parts of Arizona and southern Florida) may host some monarchs year-round. These populations even breed throughout the winter on a few native and nonnative evergreen milkweed species.

MEXICO

CALIFORNIA

# MONARCH LOOK-ALIKES

With their striking wing pattern and bold colors, monarchs (*Danaus plexippus*) are one of the easiest butterflies to recognize; however, there are a few look-alikes that can fool you.

**THE VICEROY** (*Limenitis archippus*) is the most similar-looking butterfly you might encounter. This is probably no accident—viceroys and monarchs are thought to have evolved as "co-mimics" to reinforce that they taste bad when encountered by birds or other potential predators (see page 27). The best way to tell viceroys from monarchs is to look for a black bar that crosses the wing veins on their hind wings. Monarchs lack this black bar. Viceroys are usually a bit smaller than monarchs. Viceroys' range overlaps with that of monarchs east of the Cascade and Sierra Nevada mountains.

**THE QUEEN** (*Danaus gilippus*) is closely related to the monarch and can be easily confused with it. Unlike monarchs, queens have white spots on their hind wings and are typically darker in color. Their eggs and caterpillars are nearly identical to monarchs' and trickier to distinguish—but queen caterpillars have three sets of protuberances (filaments that resemble antennae). Monarchs have only two sets.

**THE SOLDIER** (*Danaus eresimus*), another close relative, is slightly smaller than the monarch and a somewhat darker orange. Like the queen, soldiers have a few white spots on the borders of the hind wings. Both soldiers and queens occasionally wander north into the central United States, but they are primarily residents of warm regions such as Texas, Florida, the Southwest, Mexico, Central America, the Caribbean, and beyond.

# Shrinking Populations

Through ongoing monitoring efforts, scientists are able to accurately estimate the overall size and trend of monarch populations each year. This takes place when the butterflies are grouped and stationary at overwintering sites.

One of these monitoring programs is coordinated by the World Wildlife Fund–Mexico. It measures the size (in hectares) of the area occupied by monarchs within the Monarch Biosphere Reserve, which includes the largest monarch overwintering sites in North America. The second program, in California, is the Xerces Society's Western Monarch Thanksgiving Count—a community-based monitoring project in which volunteers count monarchs at hundreds of overwintering sites.

The data from these efforts suggest that the number of Eastern monarchs overwintering in Mexico declined by approximately 80 percent between the mid-1990s and 2010s. The western population has likewise been falling for years and underwent a major population crash in 2018—an estimated decline of over 99 percent since the 1980s. While populations may increase or decrease from year to year (usually due to weather), the long-term trend for this butterfly is steeply downward.

Fueled by the information gathered through these long-term monitoring efforts, in 2014 Xerces and its conservation partners (including the Center for Biological Diversity, the Center for Food Safety, and Dr. Lincoln Brower) determined that action was needed. In response, the coalition petitioned the US Fish and Wildlife Service to protect the monarch as a threatened species under the Endangered Species Act (ESA). As of this writing, the question of ESA protection for the monarch still remains under consideration. Protection under the ESA is a powerful tool for a species' recovery.

## Habitat Loss

The loss of milkweed is one of the most significant forces driving the plunge in monarch numbers. Over the past 25 years, an expansion of corn and soy production and a corresponding increase in herbicide use have reduced the abundance of milkweeds and nectar plants. Mowing and spraying of roadsides and fencerows also contribute to the loss of monarch habitat.

Ever-expanding urban and suburban development threatens monarch habitat as well, as does the spread of invasive plants such as reed canary grass and cheatgrass.

At overwintering sites in Mexico, illegal logging degrades the forest microclimate that monarchs require. In coastal California, development and a lack of appropriate management have degraded and destroyed areas where monarchs overwinter.

## Insecticides

In recent years, the class of insecticides known as neonicotinoids has received attention for risks to pollinators. Part of the appeal, and concern, of neonicotinoids is that they are generally long-lived and systemic in nature. As such, they are absorbed into plant tissue, where they linger as a built-in chemical defense against pests. Monarchs feeding on an intentionally or accidentally treated plant could be exposed to a harmful dose.

Although neonicotinoids are the most commonly used class of insecticides, others (diamides, sulfoximines, and butenolides) share many of the same traits and are increasingly used in both urban and agricultural landscapes.

### NURSERY ALERT

Nursery plants may be treated with pesticides because of consumer expectations for perfect, insect-free plants. Regulations, aimed at minimizing the spread of pests across state lines, sometimes also require nurseries to use pesticides. Consequently, toxic levels of insecticides have been repeatedly detected in plants sampled from garden centers and nurseries.

Although many native plant nurseries use few or no insecticides, when you are shopping it is good practice to ask whether or not the plants have been treated with insecticides. If they have been treated, or if the nursery owner does not know, we recommend not buying them.

## Climate Change

Most likely, climate change is already impacting monarchs with more frequent episodes of severe weather, particularly during the winter when the butterflies cluster in trees for protection from rain and wind. Changing climate also threatens the trees and forests used for overwintering.

Other plant species, such as milkweeds, may also experience increased hardship under a warmer climate. As one example, the nonnative oleander aphid (*Aphis nerii*), a detrimental herbivore pest of milkweed (see pages 54 to 55), is most common in warm regions, like California and Texas (although it does appear in northern states during summer). Under a scenario of hotter, longer summer conditions, this invasive insect may become more numerous, widespread, and destructive.

Indeed, scientists predict that some crop pests may also become more common under warmer conditions. In turn, this may lead to increases in pesticide use, a trend that would be detrimental to all wildlife.

While it may be possible to forecast some of the impacts of climate change on monarchs, other effects are less clear. For example, warmer temperatures are known to speed up caterpillar development time. Altered climate conditions may also expand the range of some plant species northward and into higher elevations. The consequences of these kinds of changes are difficult to predict.

## Biological Threats

As the monarch population shrinks, biological threats such as parasites, diseases, and invasive predators have become more significant. For example, although the impact of predators on monarchs is poorly understood, researchers believe predation to be an increasing problem, especially due to the spread of nonnative species such as the red imported fire ant (*Solenopsis invicta*). Additional concerns are arising about the protozoan parasite *Ophryocystis elektroscirrha* (OE), which seems to thrive on nonnative tropical milkweed, an issue described later in this chapter (see pages 28 to 29).

## Captive-Rearing and Mass Releases

Because people find butterflies beautiful and fascinating, it's not surprising that demand continues to exist for commercially reared monarchs that can be purchased for mass release at weddings and other events. This practice is not a conservation strategy, however, and can introduce diseases and different genetics to wild monarchs. Thus, the conservation community strongly discourages this practice.

What about captive-rearing monarchs at your home? Raising a few individuals—such as keeping a handful of locally collected caterpillars where kids can observe them and contribute to community science efforts—probably presents few risks. However, captive-rearing does not address the habitat problems that monarchs face and, if done on a large scale, could introduce more risks to an already struggling species.

If you choose to rear monarchs, consider these issues and how to approach them:

**ISSUE:** Captive-rearing of monarchs can increase disease and promote inbreeding.

**APPROACH:** To minimize this, collect monarch eggs or caterpillars locally, and release adults shortly after they emerge. Do not keep monarchs in captivity for breeding or for long periods of time. Take precautions to sanitize rearing containers. Learn to test monarchs for the parasite OE, and don't release any infected monarchs into the wild.

**ISSUE:** Captive-reared butterflies may be less successful at migrating because the cues they sense and use for migration are different indoors than in the wild.

**APPROACH:** A better solution than bringing monarchs indoors is to place a mesh cage over a milkweed plant in your garden to protect it from predators.

**ISSUE:** Captive-rearing is not a good way to restore monarch populations.

**APPROACH:** Support monarch conservation by creating habitat, reducing pesticide use, contributing to community science projects, and advocating for monarchs!

## A Monarch's Menu

Despite the many threats that monarchs face, there are things that everyone can do to help secure a better future for these butterflies. Restoring habitat, the central focus of this book, is the obvious and most important step.

Considering their size, monarch caterpillars eat a stunning amount. In just a matter of two weeks, a single caterpillar may eat several hundred times its original weight in foliage, growing to more than 2,000 percent of its size as a hatchling. Unlike the star of Eric Carle's classic book *The Very Hungry Caterpillar*, however, monarch caterpillars cannot eat everything. They eat only one kind of food, and that food is milkweeds.

To us, depending on a single food source may sound both risky and endlessly boring. Fortunately, there are approximately 75 native milkweed species in Canada and the United States, and monarch larvae can digest most of these, so they have some options for dietary diversity. Of these milkweed species, some are common and widespread, while others are quite rare.

Depending on the milkweed species and the size of its leaves, a single caterpillar might eat 4 to 20 leaves during its development. In the case of small milkweeds with narrow leaves, a single plant may be enough to feed only one caterpillar.

## Fuel for the Future

Interestingly, the massive feeding that monarchs do as caterpillars isn't just about powering their larval growth. Caterpillars also need to eat for the butterflies they will become. This is particularly true for the production of eggs, which are made almost entirely of protein. As adults, monarchs feed on sugary flower nectar as a source of carbohydrate fuel, giving them the energy to keep flying during their long migration. Much of the protein they need to make eggs, however, probably comes from the leaf feeding they do as caterpillars, and the protein reserves they store up in that life stage.

The nectar of wildflowers such as common milkweed (left) and seaside goldenrod (right) fuels the monarch's long journeys.

As you watch caterpillars feeding on your own milkweed plants, you might notice that during their smallest early-instar phases, monarch caterpillars feed in a tell-tale **trenching** pattern—not chewing all the way through the leaf. Later, as late-instar caterpillars, they may consume not only entire leaves but also flower buds and other parts of the plant.

## Protective Poison

Along with the plant proteins monarchs accumulate from feeding, milkweed supplies caterpillars with protective **cardenolides**—the toxic compounds that make them unpalatable to many predators. Over millions of years of shared adaptation and evolution, milkweeds have produced these bitter compounds as a defense against being eaten, while monarchs have countered by developing a tolerance to the toxins. Adult monarchs advertise the toxicity they gain from milkweeds through their wings' bright, black-orange-white warning coloration, intended to signal "Watch out! I'm poisonous."

## Flying on Sugar

As adult butterflies, monarchs feed on nectar from a wide variety of blooming plants. Nectar, which is usually around 10 to 70 percent sugar, provides not only critical carbohydrates but also water and low levels of amino acids, lipids, and proteins, as well as vitamins and minerals. This fuel source supplies the energy for breeding, migrating, and overwintering.

The quality and quantity of nectar sources may play an important role in the size of monarch populations. Spring-blooming flowers fuel the spring migration (especially in southern states and California), summer bloomers sustain breeding monarchs across the northern edge of their range, and fall bloomers supply some of the lipids (fats) that will fuel the long journey to overwintering sites. In both Mexico and California, winter-blooming flowers are valuable to help sustain monarchs through the winter.

## COLOR PREFERENCES

Monarchs have a broad visual spectrum and true color vision. This allows them to locate nectar plants in the landscape. You may have heard that monarchs prefer orange, yellow, and red flowers, such as various goldenrods and sunflowers, but they will eagerly nectar at blue, pink, purple, and white flowers as well. They are known to switch allegiance to a particular flower color if it provides a better nectar reward. Although monarchs may have preferences, they are very opportunistic—they'll feed on what's available.

## Junk-Food Diets

Monarchs visit more than 470 different flower species in the United States—including milkweeds, which make up about a third of all nectaring observations reported. This demonstrates the unique value of these plants to monarchs during all their life stages.

Despite being promoted as "monarch friendly," nonnative milkweeds are a potential problem for these butterflies. Tropical milkweed (*Asclepias curassavica*), often sold under varietal names like 'Silky Gold' or 'Red Butterfly', is the most common of these, although milkweed relatives such as balloon plant (*Gomphocarpus physocarpus*) and swan milkweed (*G. fruticosus*) may also show up in nurseries.

These plants are eagerly accepted as food sources by monarch caterpillars. The concern is that in areas with mild winters, such as coastal California and the Gulf states, the plants stay evergreen rather than die back to the ground in the fall as most native milkweeds do. This extended season of caterpillar food sources means some monarchs will stay and lay eggs rather than migrate to their overwintering grounds.

Winter breeding on tropical milkweed can result in poor caterpillar development and a high rate of infestation by the protozoan parasite known as OE (*Ophryocystis elektroscirrha*), which accumulates on the leaves of nonnative evergreen milkweeds. Although OE is found on native milkweeds as well, the parasite can reach unusually high levels on nonnative evergreen milkweeds in the fall and winter because these species do not drop their leaves and, hence, do not drop their OE spores.

Plants and butterflies infected with OE can also spread disease to future generations and next season's monarchs as they return from their overwintering grounds, further fueling the spread of OE in the population. For this reason, we highly recommend avoiding these nonnative milkweeds in gardens; instead, use native milkweeds and nectar plants.

## NOT ALL HOST PLANTS ARE GOOD HOSTS

In addition to tropical milkweed and balloon plant, three other nonnative milkweed relatives are a source of concern for two reasons: They are poor host plants and they are invasive. Black swallow-wort (*Cynanchum louiseae*), European swallow-wort (*C. rossicum*), and white swallow-wort (*C. vincetoxicum*) all originated in southern Europe but have escaped and spread across parts of the Northeast, Midwest, and the West.

While these invasives crowd out other native plants, they also confuse monarchs with plant chemistry that is similar, but not identical, to that of true milkweeds. Caterpillars trying to feed on these plants won't successfully develop into adult butterflies and are likely to die.

Left to right: Black swallow-wort, European swallow-wort, white swallow-wort

# 2

# Creating *and* Protecting Monarch Habitat

**The existence of a book on gardening for monarchs, and of motivated readers like you, is something of a miracle. Only a few decades ago, the concept of creating native plant gardens was just beginning to gain traction. Fortunately, with wider awareness, the movement has grown.**

Today there's an unprecedented interest in pollinator gardens and native wildflowers. Books, classes, landscape professionals, and websites are easily available to support anyone with the interest and motivation to redesign their outdoor spaces to provide functional and beautiful habitat for butterflies (and a myriad of other fascinating creatures). Using this trove of native plant gardening information, more and more of us are transforming monotonous lawns into color-filled meadows, and urban streets into nectar corridors of flowering bioswales, green roofs, and sidewalk forests of native shade trees.

Beyond just monarchs, these kinds of native plant greenspaces provide valuable habitat for hundreds of other butterfly species, as well as moths, native bees, vast numbers of other insects, and all the creatures that feed on those insects—frogs, birds, bats, and even larger insect eaters such as foxes. Locally native plants also require little to no supplemental water or fertilizer after establishment and typically don't need extensive maintenance beyond occasional weeding, thinning, pruning, or annual mowing.

While this book focuses on plants rather than on the planting process, some fundamentals of habitat creation are worthy of mention here.

## Timing Plants to the Monarch Migration

If you know the basics of monarch migration, you can provide plants that are in bloom when the butterflies pass through your area.

For example, in northern states and southern Canada, early spring wildflowers typically finish flowering before monarchs arrive, although those plants certainly support other pollinators. In southern states, on the other hand, spring-blooming plants are the critical fuel source that monarchs need to continue their northward migration. Likewise, across North America, late summer- and fall-blooming plants such as goldenrod are essential food sources for monarchs making the long trek to overwintering sites.

To the extent possible, familiarize yourself with the timing of monarch arrivals and departures in your area, and provide reliable nectar sources accordingly. Keep your own records from year to year so that you can notice patterns and changes in your specific locale.

## WHERE *NOT* TO PLANT MILKWEEDS

Monarchs journey to coastal California south of Mendocino County to overwinter, not to lay eggs. Indeed, this is one area where milkweeds do not naturally occur, and establishing them in this range can potentially harm monarchs.

Planted close to the ocean, milkweed can escape hard frosts, remaining semigreen during the monarch overwintering season. With such egg-laying sites available, monarchs may continue to mate and lay eggs into the winter, thus delaying, disrupting, or preventing their natural cycle of fall dormancy.

For these reasons, it is best to avoid planting milkweed close to overwintering sites between Mendocino and Santa Barbara (a good rule is to plant more than 5 miles [8 kilometers] inland from the coast). In southern California, near overwintering sites, avoid planting milkweed (a good rule is to plant more than 1 to 2 miles [1.6 to 3.2 kilometers] inland). Instead, plant fall-, winter-, and spring-blooming native plants that will provide nectar for nearby overwintering monarchs.

Similarly, milkweed is naturally absent in the Coast Range of Oregon and west of the Cascade Mountains in Washington. In these areas, the best way to help the occasional monarch that passes through is to plant flowers that provide nectar.

# Selecting Plants

To choose the species in this book, we surveyed scientists, consulted decades' worth of natural history literature, and polled our own staff ecologists and partners. That said, this book is not by any means all-inclusive. Monarchs are amazingly adaptable and certainly visit a huge range of plants, including native and nonnative garden plants and many native wildflowers that just aren't commercially available.

### CHOOSE NATIVE PLANTS INSTEAD OF BUTTERFLYBUSH

Although monarchs feed on butterflybush (*Buddleja davidii*) nectar, this invasive plant is notorious for escaping from yards into natural areas. Now documented in 24 states, escaped butterflybush is taking up space where native plants could be growing instead.

Great alternatives to this ornamental nuisance are wild lilac/New Jersey tea (*Ceanothus* spp.), buttonbush (*Cephalanthus* spp.), sweetpepperbush (*Clethra* spp.), and joe pye weed (*Eupatorium* spp., *Eutrochium* spp.). If you are in the Southwest, look for native butterflybush species at your native plant nursery, including woolly butterflybush (*B. marrubiifolia*) or Rio Grande butterflybush (*B. sessiliflora*).

## Sources of Native Plants

The best place to get the plants listed in this book is from local or regional nurseries that specialize in native plants or seeds. They will typically have both an appropriate inventory of locally native species and staff who are knowledgeable about the ecology and biology of each plant and can advise on matching plant choices to your project site and goals.

If you aren't yet familiar with native seed companies in your area, begin with an online search, or check the website of your state's native plant society. Native plant societies are excellent sources of information for identification, use, and enjoyment of your region's plants and the wildlife they attract.

### GO LOCALLY NATIVE WHEN POSSIBLE

Ecologists refer to plants used in habitat restoration projects as "local ecotype" when they originate in close proximity to the project site. While there is no precise definition of local ecotype, in general, if you have a range of choices, select nursery plants that are responsibly produced from wild populations as close to you as possible.

For example, a native plant gardener in Milwaukee, Wisconsin, is likely to have the best success with growing common milkweed sourced from nurseries that specialize in local ecotype plants of Wisconsin and northern Illinois, rather than local ecotype plants from Ohio or Nebraska, even though common milkweed occurs in all of those regions. Local ecotype plants tend to be most adapted to local climate conditions.

## Site Considerations

Like most butterflies, monarchs are creatures of the sun. Open meadows are ideal, while shady forests are unlikely habitats except during the overwintering season. That said, partial shade conditions can still support many of the wildflowers described in this book.

Beyond focusing your habitat creation in the sunniest areas, also take the time to understand your soil conditions, soil moisture, square footage, and the aesthetic expectations of your neighbors and community. These factors will help you refine your plant selection and choose an appropriate number of plants for a given location.

Plant selection and habitat design should be informed by your local climate.

## MONARCH-FRIENDLY PLANT COMMUNITIES

Like most plants, milkweeds tend to grow in communities with other species. To create monarch-friendly gardens or habitats, it is important to provide both milkweeds for the caterpillars and nectar plants for the adults.

Milkweeds function as both caterpillar host plants and nectar plants. Yet because their flowering period ends while monarch butterflies are still nectaring and because a diversified diet is more secure, other nectar sources are essential for the insect's full life cycle.

An optimal habitat will include grasses and sedges. These fill in spaces to reduce weeds, create visual texture, and provide habitat for nesting bees, beetles, and other beneficial insects.

# Designing Strategically

Despite the growing acceptance of native plant gardens, some communities retain perceptions of them as overgrown and unsightly. Local vegetation ordinances sometimes prohibit landscaping above a certain height, and highly subjective criteria can be used to control landscaping among homeowners' associations. Demonstrating intentionality and maintaining clearly delineated boundaries around butterfly habitat can help neighbors and the public interpret this new landscaping paradigm. Several strategies can help.

**CREATE CLEAN EDGES** to define your space. In residential settings, maintaining a closely mowed perimeter around butterfly gardens will often demonstrate that the area is not neglected. Similarly, using low-growing species near sidewalks, paths, streets, and driveways can make the area more user friendly. You can even define the edges with a row of single species, such as an attractive and uniform-looking native bunch grass.

**USE RAISED PLANTERS**—especially ones of stone, cement, or metal with a clean, modern appearance—to define a butterfly habitat. Such formal structures help offset riotous plant growth.

## A SAMPLE GARDEN

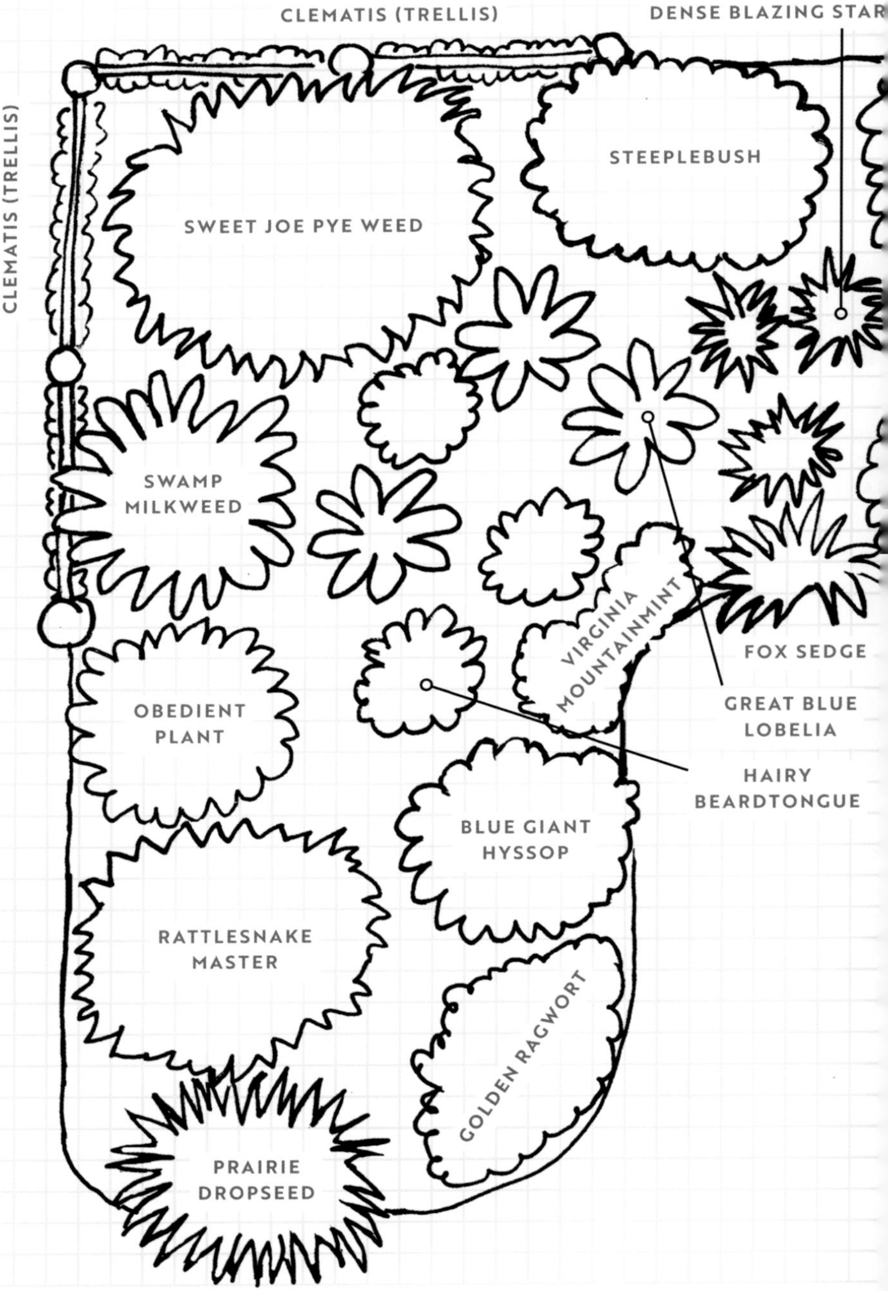

CLEMATIS (TRELLIS)
DENSE BLAZING STAR
CLEMATIS (TRELLIS)
STEEPLEBUSH
SWEET JOE PYE WEED
SWAMP MILKWEED
VIRGINIA MOUNTAINMINT
FOX SEDGE
GREAT BLUE LOBELIA
OBEDIENT PLANT
HAIRY BEARDTONGUE
BLUE GIANT HYSSOP
RATTLESNAKE MASTER
GOLDEN RAGWORT
PRAIRIE DROPSEED

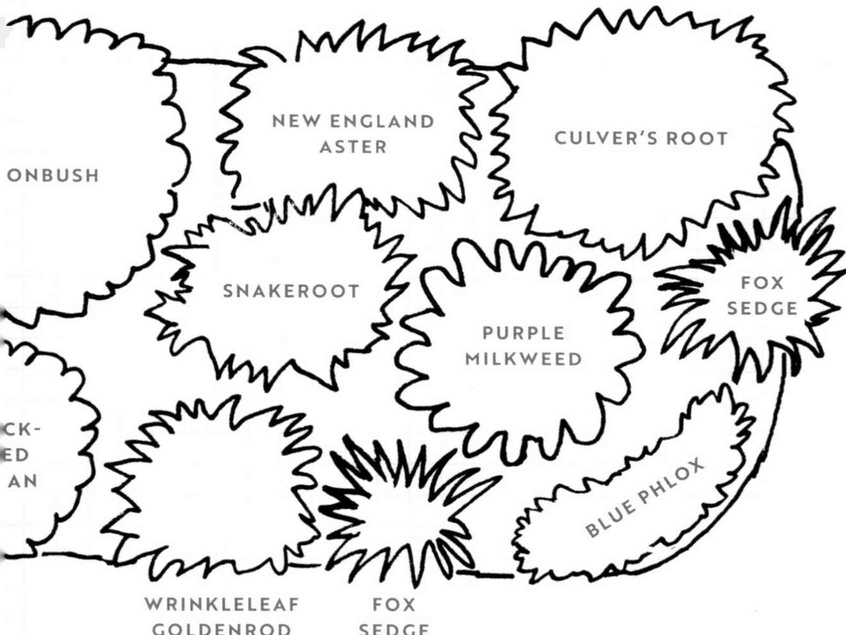

This sample monarch-garden design uses species of native wildflowers, milkweeds, and grasses that are adapted to moist soil conditions. This combination of plants will provide a sequence of flowers and color and will be attractive to both monarchs and humans throughout the growing season.

Approximately 12 feet x 20 feet (3.7 meters x 6 meters); bed 6 feet (1.8 meters) wide

**SELECT LOW-GROWING SPECIES** for public spaces, or at least species of a relatively uniform height. A number of excellent monarch plants are tall and can work well in the background. Enjoy those tall plants in the corners of a yard or establish them in fenced-off stormwater management ponds, where they'll do a good job competing with weeds.

**ERECT SIGNS** to demonstrate your intent and to educate others about butterfly habitat. Several organizations (including Xerces) offer habitat signs for native plant gardeners. For larger public spaces, consider custom signage with information about the plant species on-site and the lifecycle and migration of monarchs.

**GROUP PLANTS OF THE SAME SPECIES TOGETHER**, following a common rule of landscape designers. While not essential, such mass groupings are more likely to be interpreted as an intentional space. Landscape designers often group plants into odd numbers (three, five, seven, and so on) to provide a central focal point, although plenty of beautiful gardens depart from this rule.

**SELECT SITES PROTECTED FROM PESTICIDES** to help your plants stay free of harmful contaminants. When possible, avoid planting where you know pesticides are used. For example, the perimeters of some buildings are treated with insecticides to deter ants and termites. These treatments can persist in soils and be absorbed by the plants growing in the area. Similarly, if you know pesticides are used on an adjacent property, consider locating habitat away from that area.

## Preparing Your Site

The most daunting challenge of creating new habitat areas is often the removal of existing vegetation. Making this even tougher is the fact that most soils contain large quantities of dormant weed seeds, ready to germinate whenever bare soil is exposed.

To reduce weed pressure, we recommend not just cultivating existing vegetation and then trying to replant it with native species but suppressing weeds ahead of time as well. Successful methods include smothering the proposed planting area for a full growing season with opaque plastic or even cardboard sheets covered with wood chips. In such cases, it's fine to cultivate the soil first, creating a smooth seedbed, free of thatch and debris, before smothering. Usually, weed pressure is greatly reduced after a full growing season, and you can then uncover smothered areas.

To create pollinator habitat at a large scale, use large black tarps or clear greenhouse plastic (the latter is advantageous for transferring heat to the soil, killing some of the weed seeds). When you uncover smothered areas, if new weed seedlings do quickly appear, you can lightly rake them out (focusing on just scratching the surface) or manage them with a propane weeding torch.

The use of herbicides in habitat restoration is controversial. Give serious consideration to the unintended risks that these substances pose. At the same time, it is important to acknowledge that herbicides are usually used only for a brief period in the habitat restoration process, with the goal of re-creating a native plant ecosystem that will not be constantly exposed to future chemical use (unlike herbicides used in agriculture or turfgrass). Additionally, there continue to be new developments in organic herbicides. It is likely that continuing research and development will produce more options for organic-based weed control.

## Establishing Plants

Starting a garden directly in the ground from seed can be a low-cost way to create large habitat areas. In addition, some milkweeds and wildflowers will be available only from seed you have collected yourself or obtained from commercial sources. For successful establishment, direct seeding requires an especially clean, weed-free site. This will reduce the amount of dormant weed seed that may compete with wildflower seedlings for sunlight, space, and resources. Transplants are easier to work with than seed, but they are also more expensive.

### Seeding: Timing and Technique

In most areas, we recommend seeding in the fall, so that the cool, moist conditions of winter prepare seeds to germinate in spring. In mild climates with long summer dry seasons (such as the West Coast), this can begin as early as September if sites are clean and ready for planting. In cold climates, planting can take place late into the winter, with seed being spread even over snowy ground (known as **frost seeding**). If you are unable to plant until spring, it's a good idea to store seed in the refrigerator, since some species germinate best after prolonged exposure to cold conditions (called **cold stratification**).

When seeding, it is best to scatter seed directly onto the soil surface. A minimal dusting of soil over the seed is usually fine, but do not bury it deeply. The seeds of many wildflowers are incredibly small, and as little as a half inch (12 mm) of soil may be too deep for seedlings to germinate and grow through.

## Transplanting

Quicker to mature than seeds, transplants may be soil-bound plugs (also known as **starts**), bare-root transplants, corms or tubers, or divisions of existing perennial plants. Like seeds, transplants usually have the best survival rate when they are installed in the fall, taking advantage of winter precipitation and cool temperatures that reduce root stress. Most transplants also benefit from supplemental irrigation during the first growing season (an inch—2.5 cm—of water per week is a standard rule of thumb in most temperate climates). As with seed, by the second year, supplemental irrigation is usually unnecessary except in drought conditions.

### HOLD BACK ON MULCH

Many ornamental landscapes are established by installing wildflowers into woven landscape fabric (a plastic geotextile), as well as surrounding them with bark mulch or wood chips. Such ground covers reduce weeds, yet they also reduce the ability of native plants to spread by seed and underground rhizomes. Moreover, these ground covers can reduce the value of habitat to ground-dwelling wildlife.

Where possible, we recommend that you plant habitat areas without landscape fabric, and that you use only raked autumn tree leaves, seed-free grass clippings, or pine needles to mulch new transplants.

## Getting New Habitat off to a Strong Start

Once wildflower seeds do germinate, it is important to keep them regularly watered if there is not enough rain. Usually by the second year of growth, native plants are well adapted to grow on their own, without irrigation, under normal climate conditions.

The majority of wildflowers described in this book are perennial species that can be slow to establish from seed. Many will not flower in the first year since they are concentrating their growth into deep root systems rather than blossoms. Because of this slow growth, it is not uncommon for fast-growing annual weeds to pop up all around perennial wildflower seedlings.

A common management strategy is to mow new habitat areas, or to use a string trimmer to cut off the tops of weeds, reducing their ability to create more seed. Be sure to set the mower blade high enough to avoid damage to the typically small wildflower seedlings, while still removing the tops of the much taller annual weeds.

## Long-Term Habitat Management

Aside from routine weeding, most established meadow- or prairie-type landscapes benefit from an occasional close mowing during the dormant season (usually late fall or early winter). In general, we recommend mowing on a rotational basis, leaving at least one-third of the habitat area unmown every year. This will provide refuge for overwintering insects and other wildlife and food sources for songbirds.

This kind of rotational mowing lets you manage the amount of biomass on your site and prevents a large buildup of dead stems that may suppress new wildflower germination and growth. To further control the buildup of biomass, bag mowed plant material and remove it, or rake it into piles for removal. Note that these mowed stems can contain valuable wildflower seeds, dormant insects, the eggs of native bees, and other beneficial organisms. Rather than sending it to the landfill, or smothering it in the bottom of a compost pile, consider depositing clippings in an out-of-the-way place and allowing them to decompose naturally. This will allow any remaining insects to complete their life cycle.

## WHEN MILKWEEDS LOOK LESS THAN THEIR BEST

In their prime, milkweeds are tremendously attractive plants. At times, though, they can look less than their best, and it's useful to know why.

**DEFOLIATION.** If milkweed leaves are chewed, leaving holes, rough edges, or no leaves at all, it usually means that things are going really well: Monarch caterpillars (or other types of insects) are feeding on them. View them from that perspective and feel good.

**APHIDS.** Aphid infestations can occasionally tax and weaken the milkweed plant. If this concerns you, a gentle way to reduce the aphids is by knocking them off with your fingers. Aphids can quickly reproduce by cloning themselves, and they are tiny enough to escape detection, so aim for the realistic expectation that you will never entirely eradicate them.

**FALL COLOR.** Milkweeds are perennial plants, and most species go dormant over the winter. The leaves will start to dry, turn yellow, and drop as summer shifts to fall and winter. This is part of the natural senescence (aging process) and life of a milkweed.

## Avoiding Pesticide Use

The impacts of pesticides—which by definition include insecticides, herbicides, fungicides, and other poisons—can be highly variable. For example:

- Most insecticides can kill beneficial and pest insects alike.
- Some insecticides may not directly kill insects but can compromise cognition, mating, and development.
- Herbicides may kill, stunt, or delay flowering of plants that monarchs and other pollinators need.
- Even fungicides can negatively impact immune health, development, and reproduction of some insects.
- Some fungicides may also work synergistically with certain insecticides to make them more potent.

Given these various risks, we recommend never using pesticides for purely aesthetic reasons, and to use them only with extreme caution in established wildlife habitat. As a rule, there should never be a need to apply insecticides to butterfly habitat.

Note that a few nonnative insects will also feed on milkweeds, including Japanese beetles and oleander aphids (the latter can be especially destructive, both weakening plants and spreading plant diseases). Even in these cases we recommend that you accept some damage or find alternative methods to manage pests.

Given enough time, ecological systems tend to find a new balance in which native predatory insects evolve to prey upon these pests. That process can be remarkably fast or slow, depending on individual circumstances. In any case, attempting to control these pests with insecticides will not make the slightest dent in their global populations but will simply expose lots of harmless and helpful insects to unnecessary poisons.

**As a rule, there's no good reason to apply insecticides to butterfly habitat.**

PART II

# The Plants Monarchs Need

In the sections ahead, we present 34 of the more common, celebrated, and important monarch host plants. We also highlight 66 of the most notable and beautiful wildflowers, shrubs, and trees that sustain monarchs with nectar during their remarkable, free-flying adult life.

**NAMING.** For each group, the plants are organized alphabetically by common name, followed by the scientific name. We've largely used the plant-naming conventions established by the USDA's PLANTS database; however, in cases where the taxonomy is undergoing reorganization, we've included multiple variants.

**RANGE MAPS.** This book is written to cover the entire monarch range within the contiguous United States and southern Canada. Maps show the general distribution for each plant group; individual species may have a smaller range than their respective larger plant group. In some cases, certain species might be rare within the illustrated range.

In some of the maps you'll notice a dashed line across southern Canada and/or the Pacific Northwest. This indicates the approximate limit of the monarch's range, with that particular plant's range continuing northward.

**ADDITIONAL INFORMATION.** The profiles we've developed also include optimal locations for each type of plant, sun exposure preferences, soil moisture requirements, bloom period, flower color, height, and commercial availability.

**ORGANIZATION.** Among the milkweed profiles, we include not only species that are showy, easy to grow, and widely available from nurseries but also some that are less showy, hard to grow, and downright rare. For the former group, we are able to provide a bit more information, including a list of suggested companion plants to guide readers in rounding out their gardens or plantings with other native species. For the latter, less familiar species, we include the modest information that we do have in the hope that these wonderful milkweeds get some overdue attention.

The nectar plants are organized in two groups: wildflowers (forbs), and woody plants (trees, shrubs, and a vine). Each nectar plant group offers a general description, followed by recommended species within that group. Because most people are interested in butterflies beyond just monarchs, we've also listed other butterflies (and some showy moths) that feed on these plants.

# 3
# The Extraordinary Milkweed

What makes a milkweed a milkweed? The *milk* part of the name is generally evident: These plants produce a thick white latex as a defensive compound. But there are exceptions. Not all milkweeds have this milky sap, butterfly milkweed being one example. As for *weed*, that term can be understood as an older name for plants that grew spontaneously, without being planted.

Roughly 75 milkweed species are native to North America and another 30 or so to Central and South America, all classified together in the genus *Asclepias*. This name comes from Aesculapius, the ancient Roman god of medicine, and was assigned to milkweeds by Karl Linnaeus because the plants were known and used by folk healers. Along with thousands of other plant species, milkweeds are members of the dogbane family (Apocynaceae/Asclepiadaceae).

## Milkweed Leaves

The foliage of milkweed species is remarkably diverse, ranging from bright green to dark gray, with textures from downy to waxy. Shapes can be narrow and needlelike, tapering, broad and rounded, clasping, or heart-shaped.

Milkweed leaves can also be arranged on a plant stem in three ways: opposite (a pair of leaves growing at the same point on the stem, directly across the stem from each other); alternate (a single leaf growing from the stem, with no leaf in the same position directly across the stem); and whorled (three or more leaves attached to the stem at the same point, each radiating outward).

Common milkweed (*Asclepias syriaca*) with opposite leaves (a pair of leaves together at the same point, each going in the opposite direction)

Green antelopehorn (*A. viridis*) with alternate leaves (a single leaf by itself at each point along the stem, each leaf going in its own direction to reach and capture sunlight)

Whorled milkweed (*A. verticillata*) with whorled leaves (three or more leaves attached to the stem at the same point, each radiating outward)

### Latex

Nearly all milkweed species produce the milky latex fluid—primarily in the leaves, but also in the stems. The sticky nature of wet latex can clog the mouths of chewing caterpillars, but it also provides the cardenolide compounds that are toxic to many monarch predators.

## Milkweed Flowers

Beyond latex, another defining and unifying characteristic of milkweeds is their flowers. These are grouped in clusters; each cluster is an **umbel** of multiple flowers on individual stems radiating out from a central base.

In order for pollination to occur, the foraging insect's leg must slip inside a slit on the floret and pull out one or more pollen-bearing sacs, called pollinia.

## A CLOSER LOOK

A closer look at an individual blossom (magnification may be helpful) shows the unique forms and structures of a milkweed flower.

The flower parts are in sets of five. The corolla encircling the base of the flower has five petal-like lobes that are usually pointed at the tips and angled downward.

Above the corolla is the corona, which holds the reproductive parts of the flower. Within the corona, five pouchlike hoods are arranged around a central column. In most, but not all, species a horn projects from the opening in each hood and arches toward the central column. The unique structure of the corona puts milkweed flower nectar "front and center," which allows a great diversity of pollinators to access and drink it.

## How Pollination Happens

Milkweed pollen is not borne on anthers as it is with most flowers but on the paired sacs called **pollinia**. Each linked pair of pollinia is held in a **stigmatic slit**—a tiny opening between the hoods. Monarch butterflies and other pollinators visit milkweed flowers to feed on the nectar, but as they move around from flower to flower, their insect legs slip inside the slits, catching and depositing pollinia from one plant to another. Sometimes insects get their legs accidentally stuck in these tight parts of the flower and are unable to fly away.

**Pollination**, the successful transfer of pollen, leads to **fertilization**, the growth of pollen grains to fertilize ovules in the female part of the flower.

## Fruits and Seeds

The type of fruit that develops in milkweeds is called a **follicle**, a pod that, when mature, will split lengthwise along one natural fissure. Inside, a central pearly membrane is the attachment point for dozens or hundreds of seeds.

Opposite the base of the seed is the **coma**, the silky, fluffy floss that helps carry the seeds on the wind. There is an exception here, too—aquatic milkweed (*A. perennis*) relies on water to float its seeds away to new sites for germination. These seeds entirely lack the familiar fluffy coma.

# The Other Milkweed "Bugs"

In addition to monarchs, a remarkable community of other insects also feeds on milkweeds. A short list of these creatures includes iridescent blue milkweed beetles, fire-engine red milkweed longhorn beetles, caterpillars of the milkweed tussock moth, and stem weevils. Several **true bugs** (box elder bug–like critters) will cluster together in multigenerational families slurping milkweed fluids through their syringelike mouths.

Like the monarch, many of these animals display dramatic coloration to warn potential predators of the toxic milkweed chemicals absorbed through their diet. While they can be locally common, these creatures tend to reach a balance with milkweeds and with local predators (including various spiders, wasps, a few birds, and other animals that have evolved their own tolerance for cardenolide poisons!). Becoming acquainted with these other striking-looking milkweed insects is just one of the great joys of creating monarch habitat.

More familiar milkweed visitors include ants, aphids, and spiders. In summer there is always abundant life on a milkweed plant.

## Meet the Oleander Aphid

Unlike the less common native aphids that also frequent milkweeds, the nonnative pale yellow oleander aphid (*Aphis nerii*) can quickly explode in population numbers, creating massive feeding colonies. These colonies weaken smaller milkweed plants and may spread plant viruses (observable as mosaic patterns in foliage or even plant deformities).

The secret to rapid population growth by aphids is that they clone themselves: Every aphid is a fertile female who can reproduce without mating. Bizarrely, new aphids are born already pregnant, ready to add more offspring to their global community of identical sisters. Although they don't thrive in cold climates, oleander aphids can be found feeding year-round in warmer areas. As spring arrives in northern latitudes, some windborne aphids blown from those warmer regions inevitably show up nearly anywhere milkweeds grow.

Unlike native insects, oleander aphids may cause a certain amount of harm to milkweed populations, although much is still unknown about the scale and significance of their impact. Despite this, it's fine to ignore them or to encourage wild predators, such as tiny parasitic wasps, to help suppress their populations. The best way to accomplish this is to interplant milkweeds with other wildflowers, particularly species with abundant sources of nectar and shallow flower surfaces (such as mountainmint, goldenrods, asters, ceanothus, etc.).

Oleander aphids can rapidly increase into colonies of hundreds, even thousands, of identical individuals, eventually covering entire sections of a plant.

# 1. Aquatic Milkweed

## *Asclepias perennis*

As the name would suggest, aquatic milkweed is a plant of floodplains, bayous, seasonally flooded soils, marshes, cypress swamps, and wet roadside ditches. This adaptation to constantly moist soil makes it an excellent plant for stormwater management ponds, rain gardens, and other wet locations. That said, the wetland locations preferred by aquatic milkweed are often shadier, while swamp milkweed (*A. incarnata*) tends to prefer wet sites in full sun.

The foliage of aquatic milkweed shares some resemblance to poke milkweed, with slender, pointed, and smooth dark green leaves. The usually white flowers of this plant give way to very slender pods that open to reveal

| EXPOSURE | SOIL MOISTURE | BLOOM TIME |
|---|---|---|
| Sun to part shade | Wet | Spring, summer, and fall |

bare seeds lacking the tufts of floss found on other milkweeds. The lack of that floss points to the role of water, not wind, in seed dispersal. Drooping stems of aquatic milkweed are reported to root into the ground, forming new plants nearby.

## USES

**Hedgerow/screen/shade**

**Rain garden/wetland/stormwater management**

## COMPANION SPECIES

Companions with some tolerance for both shade and wet soils include buttonbush, great blue lobelia, cardinal flower, and sweet-scented joe pye weed.

## NATIVE RANGE

| FLOWER COLOR | HEIGHT | AVAILABILITY |
| --- | --- | --- |
| White, pink | 3 to 6 feet (0.9 to 1.8 m) | Variable by region |

# 2. Broadleaf Milkweed

## *Asclepias latifolia*

The leaves of broadleaf milkweed are so broad that young plants bear a slight resemblance to cabbages. As the plants grow and bloom, however, it becomes clear that they are milkweeds, with their characteristic flowers held tightly to the stem. Broadleaf milkweed is adapted to dry soils and occurs throughout the Great Plains and Southwest. There is little or no supply of seeds or plants, so in areas where this milkweed is native, we encourage you to ask your local native seed provider to offer this species.

### USES

**Neglected areas/tough sites**

**Xeriscape**

### NATIVE RANGE

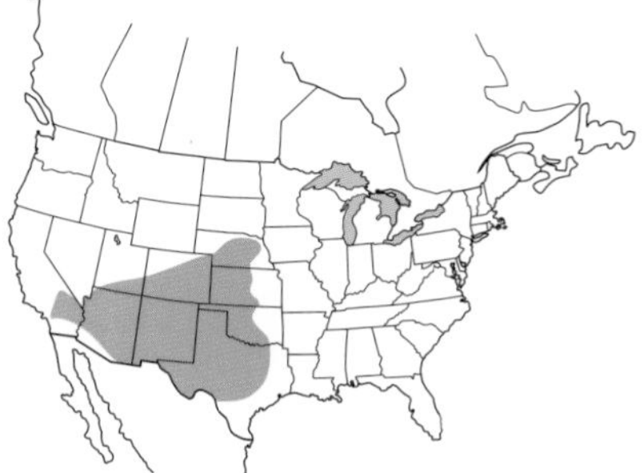

| EXPOSURE | SOIL MOISTURE | BLOOM TIME |
|---|---|---|
| Sun | Dry | Summer to fall |

| FLOWER COLOR | HEIGHT | AVAILABILITY |
|---|---|---|
| White, green, pale yellow | 1 to 3 feet (0.3 to 0.9 m) | Limited |

# 3. Butterfly Milkweed

*Asclepias tuberosa*

Of all the North American milkweeds, butterfly milkweed may be the best known as a garden plant. Its long-blooming, bright orange flower clusters and compact growth form can be incorporated into small front-yard pocket prairies and more formal ornamental gardens alike.

In natural conditions, this is a plant of sandy prairies and well-drained savannah soils where the plant's taproot mines water from many feet belowground. With care, it can be transplanted as a container-grown seedling. It prefers dry, sandy soils but can adapt to richer, more fertile soils with more moisture; excess moisture on the foliage can cause various fungal leaf spot diseases.

| EXPOSURE | SOIL MOISTURE | BLOOM TIME |
|---|---|---|
| Sun | Medium to dry | Summer |

Butterfly milkweed lacks the thick, milky latex of other milkweeds but is nonetheless very attractive to monarchs as both a caterpillar host plant and a nectar plant. The flowers are also a favorite of bumblebees.

This plant also has an interesting historical legacy. Along with common milkweed, it was once cultivated in parts of Michigan and elsewhere during the Second World War, when the seed floss was used to make buoyant life vests. Occasional large populations of the plant can still be found in areas where milkweed seed floss–processing facilities were located in states across the Great Lakes and northeastern United States.

## USES

**Ornamental**

**Containers**

**Wildflower meadow/prairie restoration**

**Neglected areas/tough sites**

## NATIVE RANGE

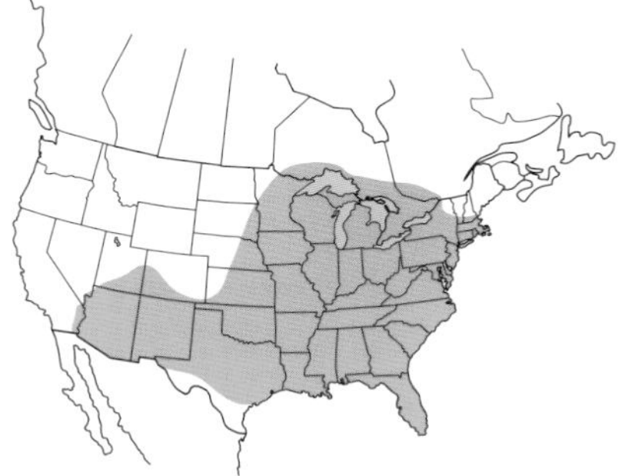

## COMPANION SPECIES

Close associates of butterfly milkweed include shorter native grass species such as little bluestem (*Schizachyrium scoparium*) and prairie dropseed (*Sporobolus heterolepis*), as well as small, shrubby wildflowers such as New Jersey tea, various coreopsis species, and spotted beebalm.

| FLOWER COLOR | HEIGHT | AVAILABILITY |
|---|---|---|
| Orange | 3 feet (0.9 m) | Wide |

# 4. California Milkweed

*Asclepias californica*

With striking dark purple flowers and fuzzy light gray foliage, this is considered by some to be California's most beautiful milkweed. Like woolly milkweed and several other species, the stems of this plant tend to lean downward and occasionally run along the ground. Companion planting with native bunch grasses can help hold the plant in a more upright position and provide a visually interesting contrast in foliage.

| EXPOSURE | SOIL MOISTURE | BLOOM TIME |
|---|---|---|
| Sun | Dry | Late spring to early summer |

Although California milkweed is mostly unavailable from nurseries, it is worth seeking out both for its appearance and because it is the earliest-emerging western milkweed. For monarchs, it may be especially important as a caterpillar host plant in the spring, before other milkweed species have emerged.

## USES

**Ornamental**

**Neglected areas/tough sites**

**Xeriscape**

## NATIVE RANGE

| FLOWER COLOR | HEIGHT | AVAILABILITY |
|---|---|---|
| Purple | 3 to 4 feet (0.9 to 1.2 m) | Limited |

# 5.
# Clasping Milkweed
## *Asclepias amplexicaulis*

If a site is dry or sandy, or has other tough soil conditions, clasping milkweed is in its favorite place. In fact, another name for the plant is sand milkweed after the soils it is adapted to. Because sand is low in moisture and fertility, these milkweeds don't grow to be large or robust and don't do well when closely planted with companion plants.

Resembling floral fireworks, the flower cluster is open and drooping, with pale purple hoods and brown-green corollas. Once the flowers are pollinated, the fruit begins to form on a stalk that points downward but then arches back to upright. The broad leaves have wavy, undulating edges and pink veins, and as the common name implies, the leaf pairs meet at the bases and encircle or clasp the stem.

This milkweed is not widely available, but it stays small and slender and is a striking focal point in gardens with dry or low-nutrient soils in the eastern United States.

### USES

**Neglected areas/tough sites**

**Xeriscape**

### NATIVE RANGE

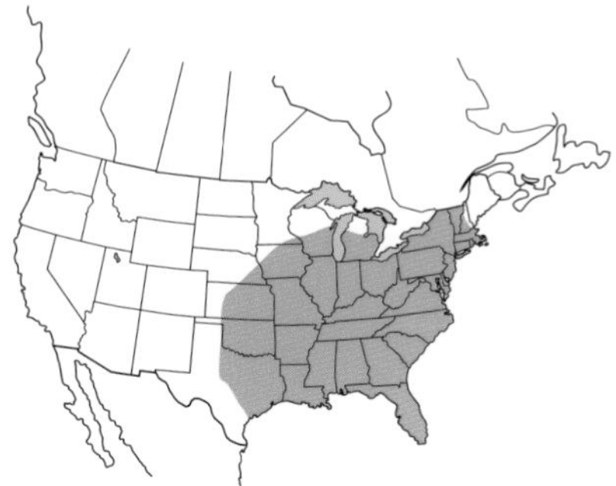

| EXPOSURE | SOIL MOISTURE | BLOOM TIME |
|---|---|---|
| Sun | Dry to very dry (pure sand) | Early summer |

| FLOWER COLOR | HEIGHT | AVAILABILITY |
| --- | --- | --- |
| Bright to pale purple | 1 to 2 feet (0.3 to 0.6 m) | Variable by region |

# 6. Common Milkweed

## *Asclepias syriaca*

The most widespread milkweed in the eastern and central United States, common milkweed is the quintessential *Asclepias* species that many people will know. It is common because it grows well, persists under a wide range of conditions, and spreads through rhizomes. And although it is common, its importance cannot be overemphasized: In terms of biomass, it provides the majority of food for caterpillars in the Eastern monarch population.

Native to grasslands, prairies, pastures, open fields, and woodland edges, common milkweed grows wild in roadsides and field edges and successfully colonizes disturbed sites.

Common milkweed is easy to grow from seed or by transplanting. The flowers have an exceptionally sweet and uncommonly full fragrance, attractive to many other pollinators and adult monarch butterflies. The undersides of the leaves are covered in a fuzz of downy hairs. Gently lift them up and look for monarch eggs in midsummer and for caterpillars throughout the breeding season.

After the plants flower and as they age, the leaves become tougher and turn yellow. These are less attractive to monarch females looking to lay eggs on tender leaves. You can encourage tender new growth by cutting back older stems at ground level, especially in colonies that are outgrowing their space.

Common milkweed attracts many insects—monarchs, beetles, true bugs (see page 54), aphids, ants, and bees—and thus is fantastic for observation. We should celebrate and appreciate the species for being common, but not take it for granted.

| EXPOSURE | SOIL MOISTURE | BLOOM TIME |
|---|---|---|
| Sun | Average to dry | Summer |

| FLOWER COLOR | PLANT HEIGHT | AVAILABILITY |
|---|---|---|
| Pink, light purple | 3 to 6 feet (0.9 to 1.8 m) | Wide |

## USES

**Ornamental**

**Wildflower meadow/prairie restoration**

**Neglected areas/tough sites**

**Hedgerow/screen/shade**

## COMPANION SPECIES

Some native grasses and wildflowers that grow well with common milkweed are big bluestem (*Andropogon gerardii*), phlox, goldenrods, mountainmint, yellow coneflower, black-eyed Susan, wild bergamot, *Silphium* spp., prairie dropseed, asters, Culver's root, Indiangrass (*Sorghastrum nutans*), and golden alexanders.

## NATIVE RANGE

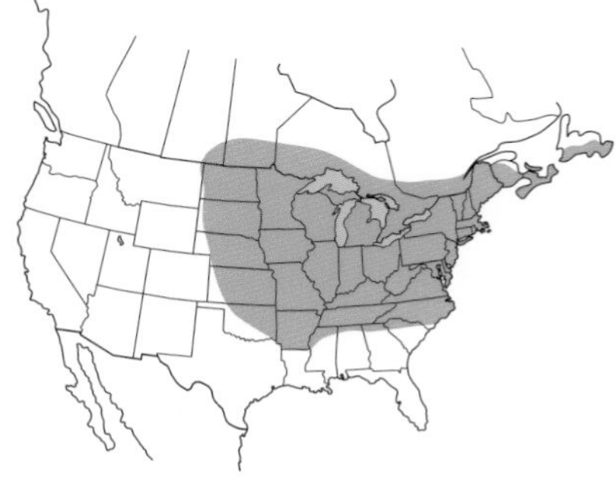

# 7. Desert Milkweed

*Asclepias erosa*

With desert milkweed, the wide range of forms and adaptations within the milkweed genus is on full display. Plants have a statuesque profile of broad leaves, held upright and overlapping, topped with dense, pale green-yellow blossoms. The leaves are a silvery pale green. Desert milkweed is adapted to parts of the Baja California Peninsula and the dry, inland areas of southern California, Arizona, and Nevada. Except for winter, desert milkweed is in flower much of the year, making it a great nectar plant for arid gardens and locations.

| EXPOSURE | SOIL MOISTURE | BLOOM TIME |
|---|---|---|
| Sun | Dry | Spring, summer, and fall |

## USES

**Ornamental**

**Neglected areas/tough sites**

**Xeriscape**

## NATIVE RANGE

## COMPANION SPECIES

Compatible with desert milkweed are manzanita, sagebrush (*Artemisia* spp.), wild lilac, native thistle, wild rye (*Elymus* spp.), gumweed, lupine (*Lupinus* spp.), pine (*Pinus* spp.), oak (*Quercus* spp.), blue dicks, and tomcat clover.

| FLOWER COLOR | HEIGHT | AVAILABILITY |
| --- | --- | --- |
| Green, yellow | 1 to 3 feet (0.3 to 0.9 m) | Limited |

# 8. Fewflower Milkweed

*Asclepias lanceolata*

As the name suggests, fewflower milkweed has slightly fewer flowers in its blooming clusters than other milkweed species offer. It makes good use of those blossoms, however, with striking red-orange flowers that resemble the color of butterfly milkweed (*A. tuberosa*).

This is a plant of freshwater swamps, brackish marshes, and wet pine forests. Due to this habitat adaptation, along with its tall upright growth form, the fewflower milkweed can be an excellent feature in rain gardens and other wet locations, where it combines well with rushes, sedges, and emergent wetland grasses.

## USES

**Ornamental**

**Rain garden/wetland/stormwater management**

## NATIVE RANGE

| EXPOSURE | SOIL MOISTURE | BLOOM TIME |
|---|---|---|
| Sun | Wet | Summer |

| FLOWER COLOR | HEIGHT | AVAILABILITY |
| --- | --- | --- |
| Orange | 3 to 6 feet (0.9 to 1.8 m) | Limited |

# 9.

# Green Antelopehorn

## *Asclepias viridis*

Also known as green milkweed (which is a common name for *A. hirtella* as well), this is one of the most familiar milkweeds in the southern Great Plains and lower Mississippi River valley. Its common and widespread distribution is testimony to the plant's very adaptable nature: It grows with relative ease even in poor soils with little organic matter, in sand, or even occasionally in rocky ground. This adaptability allows it to survive in pastures and rangelands, where cattle tend to avoid it, as well as in roadside ditches and vacant lots.

| EXPOSURE | SOIL MOISTURE | BLOOM TIME |
| --- | --- | --- |
| Sun | Medium to dry | Summer |

Even though it may not always occur in the most glamorous locations, this is an excellent ornamental garden plant with interesting flowers, variable leaf shapes, and a compact and tidy form. The small size of green antelopehorn allows it to function nicely as a bedding plant in small garden spaces and even along edges and walkways where smaller plants might be preferable.

Green antelopehorn produces descending taproots, making it well adapted to drought, as well as short horizontal rhizomes that occasionally send up a new plant shoot nearby. This is generally one of the easiest milkweeds to grow from seed and care for.

## USES

**Ornamental**

**Wildflower meadow/prairie restoration**

**Neglected areas/tough sites**

## COMPANION SPECIES

In garden settings, colorful monarch nectar plants of similar height that tolerate the same sandy or somewhat rocky soil conditions include showy penstemon, annual blanketflower, and pale purple coneflower.

## NATIVE RANGE

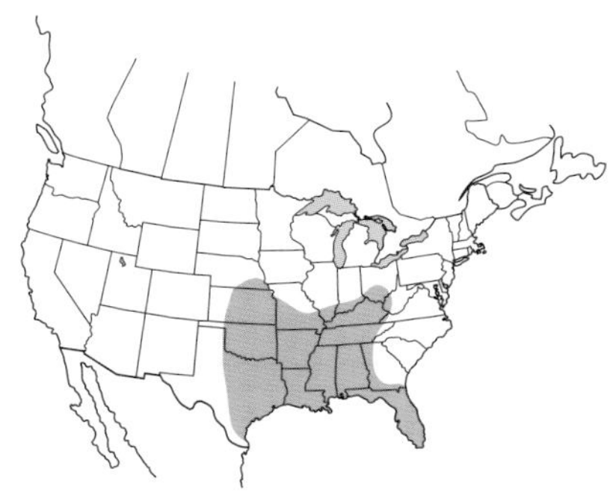

| FLOWER COLOR | HEIGHT | AVAILABILITY |
|---|---|---|
| Green, purple | 1 to 3 feet (0.3 to 0.9 m) | Wide |

# 10. Green Comet Milkweed

*Asclepias viridiflora*

Although the native range for green comet milkweed covers much of the United States east of the Rockies, it is not a common plant: In fact, it has protected status in New York, Connecticut, and Florida. This species does not tolerate competition or disturbance and so is found in remnant communities of dry or rocky grasslands. The plants grow individually and don't form colonies. The flowers are green, lack horns, and hang from the stem in drooping umbels.

| EXPOSURE | SOIL MOISTURE | BLOOM TIME |
|---|---|---|
| Sun, light shade | Dry | Summer, fall |

## USES

Wildflower meadow/prairie restoration

Neglected areas/tough sites

Xeriscape

## NATIVE RANGE

**FLOWER COLOR**
Green

**HEIGHT**
1 to 3 feet (0.3 to 0.9 m)

**AVAILABILITY**
Variable by region

# 11. Green Milkweed

*Asclepias hirtella*

In this species, the younger plants have elegant stems with narrow, upward-reaching leaves, topped by moderate-size spherical clusters of electric green flowers. Over the years, green milkweeds become round, full, and bushlike. These can be used individually as accents in flower beds or throughout larger field sites. Green milkweed pods are slender and have a covering of downy hairs.

| EXPOSURE | SOIL MOISTURE | BLOOM TIME |
|---|---|---|
| Sun | Wet to moist to average | Summer |

## USES

**Wildflower meadow/prairie restoration**

**Rain garden/wetland/stormwater management**

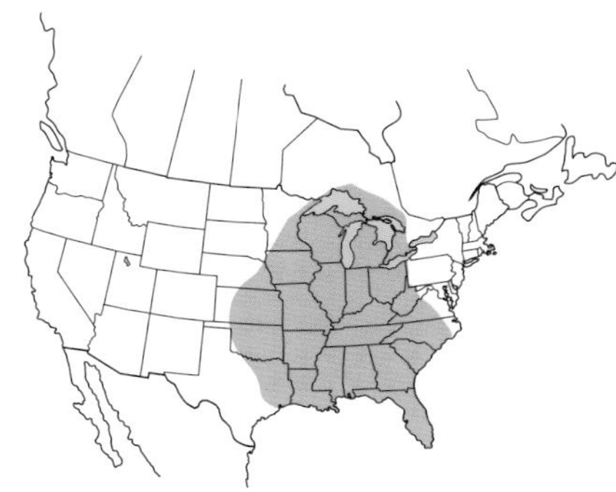

| FLOWER COLOR | HEIGHT | AVAILABILITY |
|---|---|---|
| Green | 3 to 5 feet (0.9 to 1.5 m) | Variable by region |

# 12. Heartleaf Milkweed

## *Asclepias cordifolia*

As its name suggests, heartleaf milkweed does indeed have heart-shaped leaves. The leaf tips are pointed and widen toward the base with two rounded lobes on each side of the stem where the leaf attaches. The leaves are sparsely spaced, and the growth habit is open and slightly sprawling.

Heartleaf milkweed grows wild in rocky soils and open woodlands in the Cascades and Sierra Mountains, in full sun or light shade. The pale, waxy leaves are protected against water loss under hot, dry conditions, and the purple of the veins echoes the deep reddish purple of the flowers. These flowers lack horns, and without them the lighter, almost white hoods have a smooth, lustrous, waxy appearance in contrast with the darker corollas. Each individual flower is borne on an elongated stalk, so the blossoms are open and branching.

### USES

**Containers**

**Neglected areas/tough sites**

**Xeriscape**

### NATIVE RANGE

### COMPANION SPECIES

Suitable choices include California buckeye, ceanothus, oaks, pines, manzanita, penstemon, and coyote mint.

| EXPOSURE | SOIL MOISTURE | BLOOM TIME |
|---|---|---|
| Part shade to sun | Dry | Spring and summer |

| FLOWER COLOR | HEIGHT | AVAILABILITY |
|---|---|---|
| Purple | 1 to 2 feet (0.3 to 0.6 m) | Variable by region |

# 13. Horsetail Milkweed

*Asclepias subverticillata*

Often the common names of plants are descriptive and logical. In the case of horsetail milkweed, the leaves are extremely narrow—confusingly, even more so than those of narrow-leaved milkweed (*A. fascicularis*)—and its general look is similar to horsetail plant (*Equisetum* spp.). The stems and leaves are bright green and hairless.

The plants can spread by rhizomes into sizable colonies, making horsetail milkweed best suited for large areas, naturalized yards, or xeriscape. In some rangeland areas it is considered a weed.

| EXPOSURE | SOIL MOISTURE | BLOOM TIME |
|---|---|---|
| Sun | Dry | Spring, summer, and fall |

## USES

**Wildflower meadow/prairie restoration**

**Neglected areas/tough sites**

**Xeriscape**

## COMPANION SPECIES

Good plants to grow with horsetail milkweed are other western species that also do well in tough, dry soils such as rabbitbrush, creosote (*Larrea*), wild buckwheat, lupine, vervain, gumweed, blue grama (*Bouteloua gracilis*), globe mallow, juniper, and pine.

## NATIVE RANGE

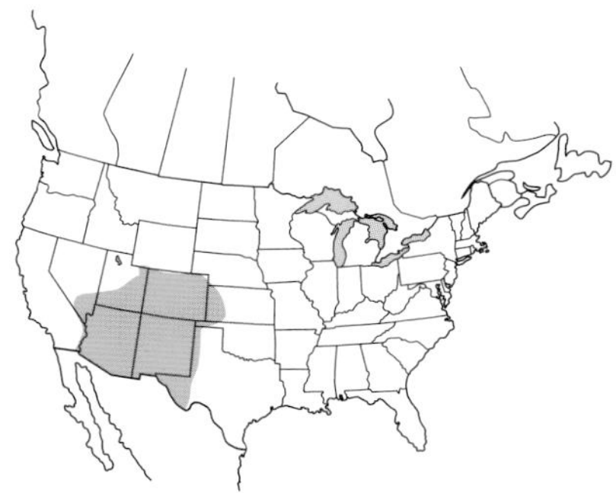

| FLOWER COLOR | HEIGHT | AVAILABILITY |
| --- | --- | --- |
| White, pale green | 0.5 to 4 feet (15 to 120 cm) | Limited |

14.

# Mexican Whorled Milkweed, Narrow-Leaved Milkweed

*Asclepias fascicularis*

Native to the western United States, Mexican whorled milkweed does well in drier sites and plays an important role in feeding growing caterpillars across the West, especially in California and Nevada. The leaves are very narrow and fold in on themselves, and they are arranged in whorls along the stem. Monarch larvae appreciate this plant and will consume many leaves and flowers.

| EXPOSURE | SOIL MOISTURE | BLOOM TIME |
|---|---|---|
| Sun | Moist to average to dry | Summer and fall |

Rather than in high-visibility areas, this species is best suited to hidden spots in the landscape, combined with other milkweeds and nectar plants. Its underground rhizomes allow it to spread clonally and resprout after heavy defoliation. It is ideal for large habitat projects because it tolerates a range of soil texture and moisture conditions, spreads easily, is excellent for monarchs, and is widely available as seeds and plants.

## USES

**Wildflower meadow/prairie restoration**

**Neglected areas/tough sites**

**Xeriscape**

## NATIVE RANGE

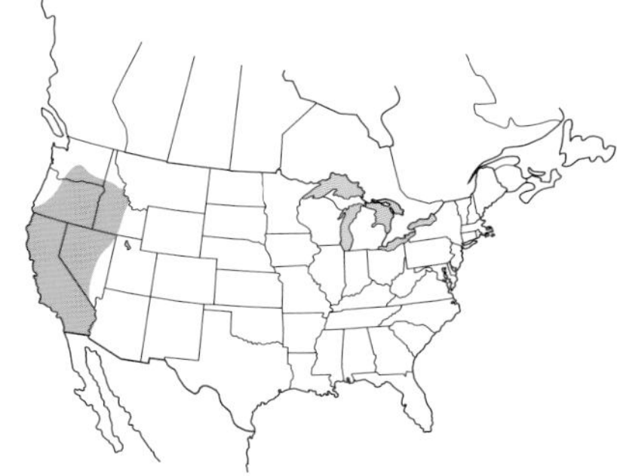

## COMPANION SPECIES

There are several groups of plants to complement Mexican whorled milkweed, including penstemon, coyote mint, desert globemallow, purple needlegrass (*Nassella pulchra*), saltgrass (*Distichlis spicata*), salvia, native thistle, wild buckwheat, and wild lilac.

| FLOWER COLOR | HEIGHT | AVAILABILITY |
|---|---|---|
| Pale pink, white | 1.5 to 3.5 feet (0.5 to 1 m) | Wide |

# 15. Oval-Leaf Milkweed

*Asclepias ovalifolia*

There are several common names for this milkweed, including oval-leaf and dwarf. It could actually be considered northern milkweed because this is the species that occurs the farthest north, centered in the upper Midwest and Dakotas and extending into southern Manitoba. This is as far north as milkweeds grow, and this distribution limits the extent of the monarch's breeding range.

| EXPOSURE | SOIL MOISTURE | BLOOM TIME |
|---|---|---|
| Sun | Average to dry | Summer |

The oval-leaf milkweed is compact with many inflorescences of white flowers. It will spread clonally, but the plants are not very tall. The availability is currently limited, but as more projects and people in its region use and seek milkweeds, the supply is increasing.

## USES

**Ornamental**

**Wildflower meadow/prairie restoration**

**Neglected areas/tough sites**

## NATIVE RANGE

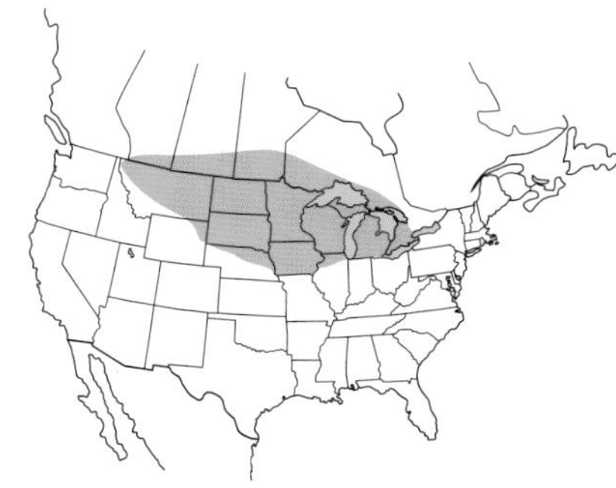

| FLOWER COLOR | HEIGHT | AVAILABILITY |
| --- | --- | --- |
| White | 1 to 3 feet (0.3 to 0.9 m) | Limited |

16.

# Pinewoods Milkweed

*Asclepias humistrata*

A sandy soil specialist, pinewoods milkweed has strikingly wide leaves with distinct purple veins, which can rightfully be described as some of the showiest foliage of any milkweed. In some plants, the foliage may appear more purple than green, with even the seedpods taking on a deep violet hue.

Despite its exotic appearance, this is a short-statured plant, one that often sprawls along the ground with an almost vinelike growth habit. Its thick taproot ensures the plant's survival in wildfire-adapted woodlands, helping it resprout from underground reserves after an area is burned. It

| EXPOSURE | SOIL MOISTURE | BLOOM TIME |
|---|---|---|
| Sun to partial shade | Dry | Spring to summer |

thrives in recently burned areas where competition from taller-growing vegetation is temporarily cleared away.

As with many taprooted species, pinewoods milkweed may be difficult to transplant and easier to start from seed directly in the ground. As the name might suggest, this is a plant of southern pinelands.

## USES

**Ornamental**

**Neglected areas/tough sites**

**Xeriscape**

## COMPANION SPECIES

Along with an overstory of longleaf pine and related species, good companions include anise goldenrod and dense blazing star.

## NATIVE RANGE

| FLOWER COLOR | HEIGHT | AVAILABILITY |
|---|---|---|
| White, purple | 1 to 3 feet (0.3 to 0.9 m) | Limited |

# 17. Poke Milkweed

## *Asclepias exaltata*

Widespread but fairly uncommon, poke milkweed is an occupant of rich, fertile soils of woodlands and woodland edges. With sparse, drooping flowers and smooth dark green leaves, it tends to be less showy than many other milkweeds and may simply blend in with surrounding shrub thickets. Despite its less showy appearance, however, it is sometimes described as one of the most fragrant milkweeds when in bloom.

Underused even in native plant gardens, this is an excellent, carefree plant for shady yards and woodland landscaping, as well as for habitat restoration of shrubby areas and shady ditches. It reportedly hybridizes with common milkweed, a surprising feat given the different habitats the two plants tend to prefer, and their very different appearance.

### USES

**Ornamental**

**Hedgerow/screen/shade**

### COMPANION SPECIES

Poke milkweed occupies the same type of habitat as wingstem and white snakeroot, two excellent monarch nectar plants that also tolerate partial shade and prefer rich soils.

### NATIVE RANGE

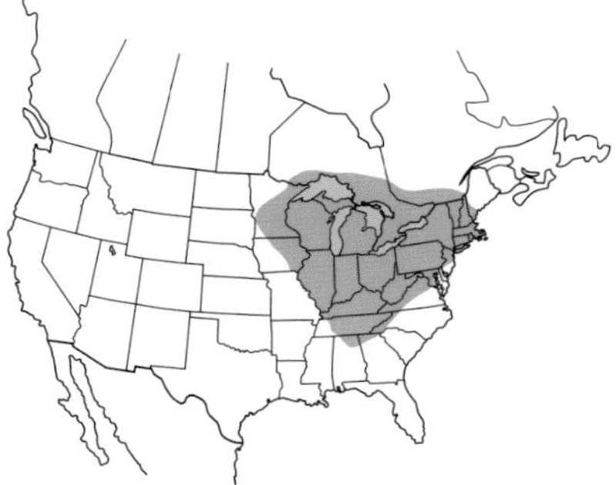

| EXPOSURE | SOIL MOISTURE | BLOOM TIME |
|---|---|---|
| Partial shade | Medium | Summer |

| FLOWER COLOR | HEIGHT | AVAILABILITY |
|---|---|---|
| White, purple | 2 to 6 feet (0.6 to 1.8 m) | Wide |

# 18. Prairie Milkweed

## *Asclepias sullivantii*

Resembling a smaller version of common milkweed, prairie milkweed is uncommon in most areas. It has long, blunt, fleshy, light green leaves with very distinct pink central veins, as well as smooth seedpods (unlike common milkweed), all of which combine to make this a showy, small-statured specimen plant.

Ecologists regard it as an indicator of high-quality habitat, and wild plants are typically found only within intact historic prairie remnants. Like common milkweed (with which it can hybridize), prairie milkweed prefers rich, fertile soils, where it builds a complex root system of both taproot and rhizomes.

| EXPOSURE | SOIL MOISTURE | BLOOM TIME |
|---|---|---|
| Sun | Medium | Summer |

Although its rhizome system does send up new shoots, it is not considered an aggressively spreading plant. That, combined with its small size, makes it a perfect substitute for common milkweed in small garden areas with limitations on space and height.

## USES

**Ornamental**

**Wildflower meadow/prairie restoration**

## NATIVE RANGE

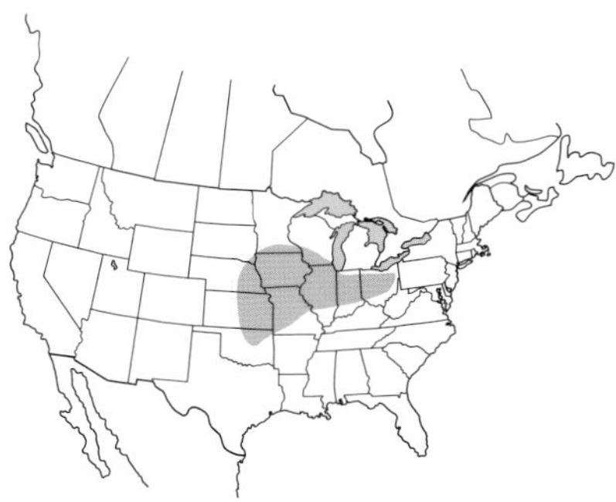

## COMPANION SPECIES

Anise hyssop and rattlesnake master combine well with prairie milkweed.

| FLOWER COLOR | HEIGHT | AVAILABILITY |
|---|---|---|
| Pink | 2 to 3 feet (0.6 to 1 m) | Wide |

19.

# Purple Milkweed

*Asclepias purpurascens*

With its vivid purple flower clusters, this milkweed can be both a garden focal point and a food source for monarch caterpillars and butterflies. Otherwise, purple milkweed is quite similar in size, form, and foliage to common milkweed (*A. syriaca*), and without the presence of flowers, it can be difficult to distinguish the two.

The leaves of purple milkweed have more pointed tips and more netted veins than common milkweed. The smooth and elongated fruits of purple milkweed also help distinguish it from common milkweed, whose fruits have a rough surface and are fuller toward the base.

| EXPOSURE | SOIL MOISTURE | BLOOM TIME |
|---|---|---|
| Partial shade to sun | Average | Late spring to summer |

Purple milkweed has rhizomes and spreads clonally but is not particularly aggressive in most locations. Rather than growing out in the open, this species is suited to woodland edges or other areas with light or partial shade rather than full sun.

## USES

**Ornamental**

**Wildflower meadow/prairie restoration**

**Hedgerow/screen/shade**

## COMPANION SPECIES

Several prairie species grow well with purple milkweed, such as big bluestem, phlox, wild bergamot, *Silphium* spp., prairie dropseed, asters, Culver's root, and mesic sedges (*Carex* spp.).

## NATIVE RANGE

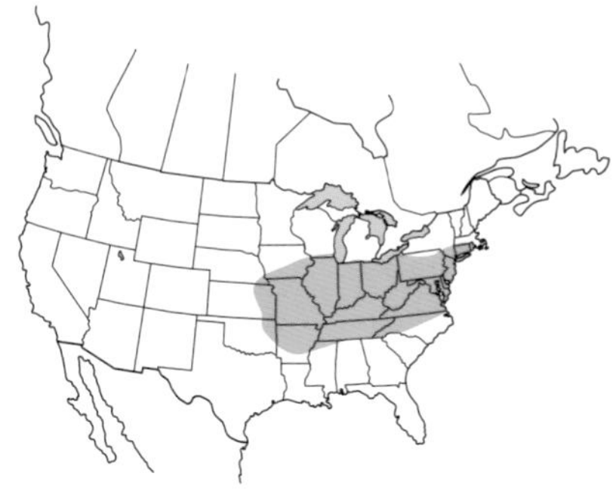

| FLOWER COLOR | HEIGHT | AVAILABILITY |
| --- | --- | --- |
| Deep pink-purple | 2.5 to 4 feet (0.7 to 1.2 m) | Wide |

# 20. Redring Milkweed

*Asclepias variegata*

This showy milkweed has dense spheres of flowers atop dark green foliage, and each white flower has a purple-red stripe encircling the junction between the corolla and corona. It is a plant of the southeastern and Atlantic states, naturally occurring in woodlands and at woodland edges.

| EXPOSURE | SOIL MOISTURE | BLOOM TIME |
|---|---|---|
| Partial shade to shade | Dry | Summer |

There is not a lot of documentation of monarch larvae feeding on this plant, which may be due to its occurrence in woodlands, while monarch butterflies prefer open habitats. It is a good plant for bees, however, and other pollinators that feed on the sweet nectar. In New York, Connecticut, and Pennsylvania, it is a rare plant in the wild and has protected status.

## USES

**Ornamental**

**Hedgerow/screen/shade**

## NATIVE RANGE

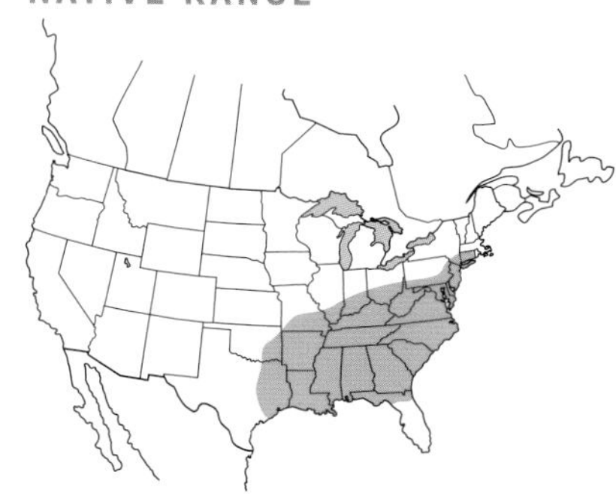

| FLOWER COLOR | HEIGHT | AVAILABILITY |
|---|---|---|
| White with purple-red ring | 1 to 4 feet (0.3 to 1.2 m) | Limited |

# 21. Rush Milkweed

*Asclepias subulata*

A true desert specialist with thick, green, almost leafless stems, this unique milkweed resembles desert succulents more than most other milkweeds. Its interesting upright stature and clumping appearance are attractive in mass plantings and formal gardens in hot desert locations. Despite its lack of leaves, we have frequently observed monarch caterpillars feeding on the stems and flower buds of this interesting species.

| EXPOSURE | SOIL MOISTURE | BLOOM TIME |
|---|---|---|
| Sun | Dry | Year-round |

## USES

**Xeriscape**

## NATIVE RANGE

| FLOWER COLOR | HEIGHT | AVAILABILITY |
|---|---|---|
| White, yellow | 3 to 5 feet (0.9 to 1.5m) | Variable by region |

# 22. Sand Milkweed

*Asclepias arenaria*

A true Great Plains milkweed, sand milkweed—also sometimes called Western sand milkweed—is native from Texas to South Dakota and east of the Rockies from New Mexico to Wyoming. The leaves are broad, with wide, blunt tips, and the flowers are green-yellow. The tight inflorescences are tucked in among the upper leaves, which have ruffled edges. The plants are upright and a great choice for dry or sandy sites.

## USES

- **Wildflower meadow/prairie restoration**
- **Neglected areas/tough sites**
- **Xeriscape**

## NATIVE RANGE

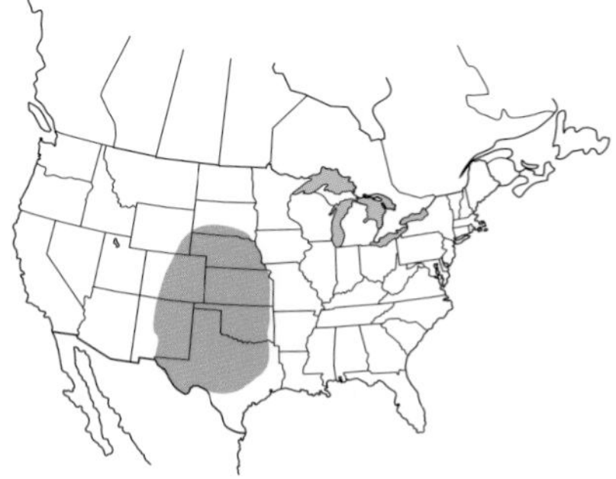

| EXPOSURE | SOIL MOISTURE | BLOOM TIME |
|---|---|---|
| Sun | Dry to very dry (pure sand) | Summer to early fall |

| FLOWER COLOR | HEIGHT | AVAILABILITY |
|---|---|---|
| Green | 1 to 4 feet (0.3 to 1.2 m) | Limited |

# 23. Savannah Milkweed

*Asclepias pedicellata*

One of the smaller milkweeds, this plant can be overlooked due to less showy flowers than those of better-known milkweeds in the same region. It is very well adapted, however, and frequently can be found in semiopen southern woodlands and, as the name suggests, pine savannahs. In natural areas, this plant probably benefits from occasional wildfires that reduce competition from larger plants, and in garden settings is best combined with other small, nonaggressive species.

## USES

**Wildflower meadow/prairie restoration**

**Neglected areas/tough sites**

**Hedgerow/screen/shade**

## NATIVE RANGE

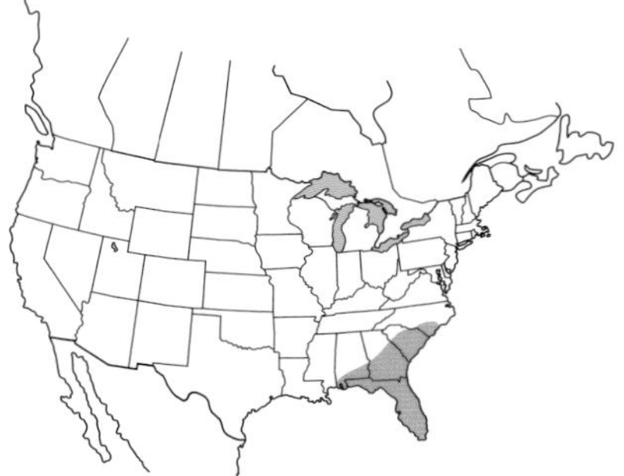

| EXPOSURE | SOIL MOISTURE | BLOOM TIME |
|---|---|---|
| Sun to part shade | Medium | Early summer |

| FLOWER COLOR | HEIGHT | AVAILABILITY |
|---|---|---|
| Yellow | 1 foot (0.3 m) | Limited |

# 24. Showy Milkweed

*Asclepias speciosa*

Unquestionably the most important "workhorse" milkweed for monarch conservation west of the Mississippi River, this is an incredibly adaptable plant. It is at home in savannahs, prairies, old fields, cold deserts, roadside ditches, and railroad edges. It also thrives in home gardens, where its large thick leaves, long bloom period, and showy flower clusters make it a fascinating and beautiful ornamental addition.

Like common milkweed, which it resembles, showy milkweed spreads by underground rhizomes to form small colonies. These colonies can become expansive in western rangeland and along roadsides, where the plant will send up lots of new stems as a survival mechanism in response

| EXPOSURE | SOIL MOISTURE | BLOOM TIME |
|---|---|---|
| Sun | Medium to dry | Summer |

to mowing. In most garden settings, it tends to remain a polite and orderly multistem clump.

At the northern end of its range, showy milkweed is typically a small plant. In warm climates, this drought-hardy species can grow much taller and produce enormous, fleshy leaves.

## USES

**Ornamental**

**Wildflower meadow/prairie restoration**

**Neglected areas/tough sites**

**Hedgerow/screen/shade**

**Xeriscape**

## NATIVE RANGE

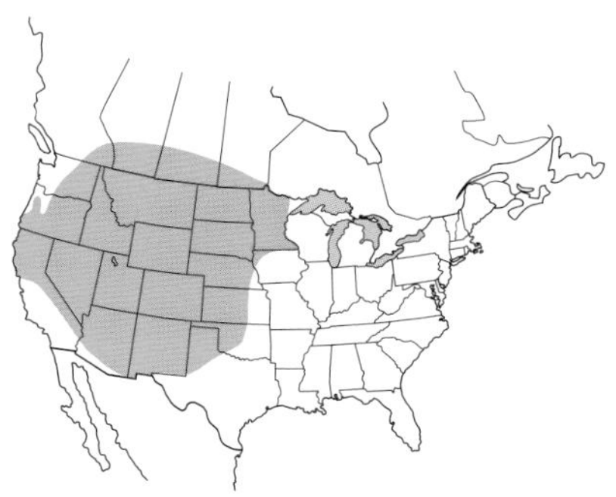

## COMPANION SPECIES

Due to its very widespread distribution, showy milkweed occurs alongside numerous other plant species in different regions. Across much of the West, it can be found among native bunch grasses such as Idaho fescue (*Festuca idahoensis*) and bluebunch wheatgrass (*Pseudoroegneria spicata*), as well as rugged dryland-adapted wildflowers such as various goldenrods and native thistles.

| FLOWER COLOR | HEIGHT | AVAILABILITY |
|---|---|---|
| Pink | 2 to 6 feet (0.6 to 1.8 m) | Wide |

# 25. Slimleaf Milkweed

## *Asclepias stenophylla*

Growing naturally throughout the central United States in dry and rocky soils, slimleaf milkweed is rare in the northern part of its range and has protected status in Illinois, Iowa, and Minnesota. The leaves are quite long and widely spaced along the stem, lending it a spindly appearance. The fruits are elongated, reaching up to 5 inches (13 cm) long.

### USES

**Wildflower meadow/prairie restoration**

**Neglected areas/tough sites**

**Xeriscape**

### NATIVE RANGE

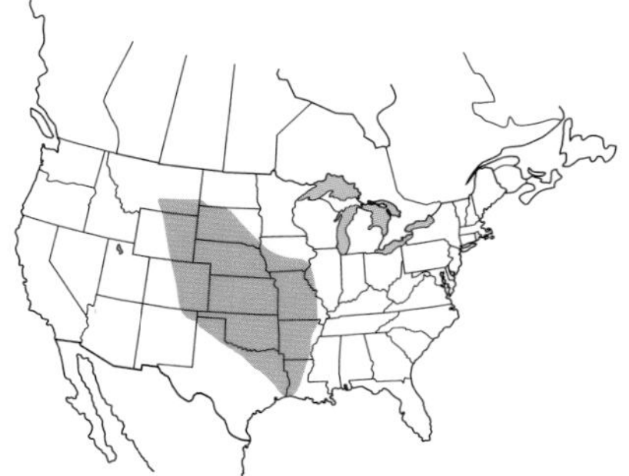

| EXPOSURE | SOIL MOISTURE | BLOOM TIME |
|---|---|---|
| Sun | Average to dry | Summer |

| FLOWER COLOR | HEIGHT | AVAILABILITY |
|---|---|---|
| White | 0.5 to 3 feet (15 to 90 cm) | Limited |

# 26. Spider Milkweed, Antelopehorns

*Asclepias asperula*

One of the first host plants that migrating monarchs encounter as they move northward every spring from Mexico is spider milkweed. This makes it particularly important from a conservation standpoint in the southern Great Plains and Texas, where monarchs typically stop to lay eggs and produce the next generation that will migrate farther north. With a clump-forming, sprawling growth habit, interesting curved pods, and large, showy flowers, this is an aesthetically interesting plant, even if the greenish flower color tends to blend in with surrounding prairie grasses.

| EXPOSURE | SOIL MOISTURE | BLOOM TIME |
|---|---|---|
| Sun | Medium | Spring to summer |

Spider milkweed is a plant of expansive rangelands and deserts, favoring rocky or sandy soils, with a long taproot system that helps the plant persist in drought and harsh growing conditions. Able to thread its root system down between rocks and hardpan, it can be difficult to transplant and may be best established in place from seed.

Despite its important conservation role, spider milkweed tends to occupy lands used for grazing, and ranchers may target it for eradication as a nuisance plant. In general, however, livestock avoid it, except in abused, overgrazed lands where more palatable options are scarce.

## USES

**Ornamental**

**Wildflower meadow/prairie restoration**

**Neglected areas/tough sites**

## NATIVE RANGE

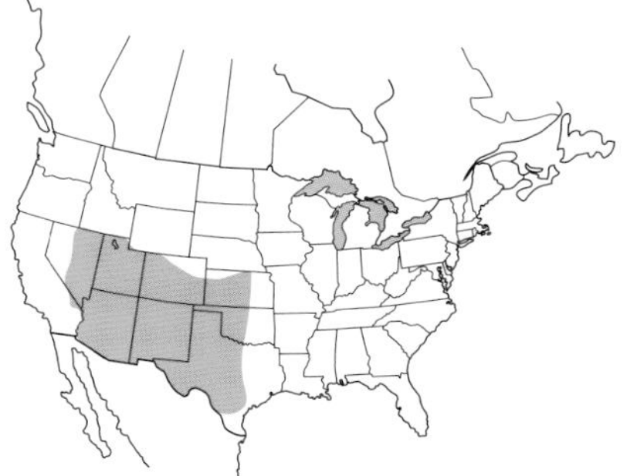

## COMPANION SPECIES

Along with native grasses such as blue grama, spider milkweed pairs well with blue sage, annual blanketflower, and lemon beebalm (*Monarda citriodora*), all of which are adapted to similar dry, stony soils.

| FLOWER COLOR | HEIGHT | AVAILABILITY |
|---|---|---|
| White, green | 1 to 3 feet (0.3 to 0.9 m) | Variable by region |

# 27. Swamp Milkweed

*Asclepias incarnata*

This is an excellent milkweed for home gardens and containers, and monarch caterpillars readily feed on it. As the common name implies, swamp milkweed grows in wet soils, but it will also do well in any reasonably moist area or regularly watered pot. It does not spread by rhizomes, so each plant stays contained, making it a great choice for flower beds. The seedpods are around 4 inches (10 cm) long and smooth green, eventually opening and turning a buff color after seed dispersal.

| EXPOSURE | SOIL MOISTURE | BLOOM TIME |
|---|---|---|
| Sun | Moist to wet | Summer |

Some white or darker pink ornamental cultivars of swamp milkweed exist, but because it is unclear which other traits (such as palatability to monarchs) may have been altered along with flower color, we recommend buying the wild-type plants.

## USES

**Ornamental**

**Containers**

**Wildflower meadow/prairie restoration**

**Rain garden/wetland/stormwater management**

## NATIVE RANGE

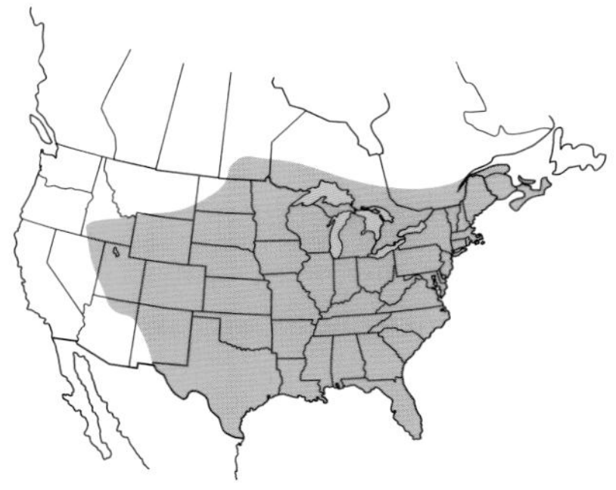

## COMPANION SPECIES

Bluejoint grass (*Calamagrostis canadensis*), upright sedge (*Carex stricta*), Virginia iris (*Iris virginica*), sneezeweed (*Helenium autumnale*), Virginia mountainmint, joe pye weed, boneset, sunflowers, swamp verbena, and marsh blazing star

| FLOWER COLOR | HEIGHT | AVAILABILITY |
| --- | --- | --- |
| Deep pink to purple | 3 to 5 feet (0.9 to 1.5 m) | Wide |

# 28. Whorled Milkweed

*Asclepias verticillata*

Relative to other milkweeds in the eastern and central United States, whorled milkweed is small and a miniature version of a milkweed in all its parts: fruits, flowers, and height. Its leaves are very narrow, with an appearance similar to bright green pine needles; each stem is slender and upright. The open flowers are pure white and also small, but a close look reveals the milkweed's characteristic hoods and coronas.

Whorled milkweed spreads by rhizomes, so it can fill in an area and usually tolerates light mowing. In fact, this is a common plant in highway and interstate medians across its range. Despite its rhizomes, the plant's small size and preference for drier soils make it a good choice for containers on balconies or patios. Best of all, whorled milkweed is a preferred and valuable host plant for monarch caterpillars: If you look closely, you may find multiple caterpillars feeding on it.

## USES

**Containers**

**Wildflower meadow/prairie restoration**

**Neglected areas/tough sites**

**Xeriscape**

## NATIVE RANGE

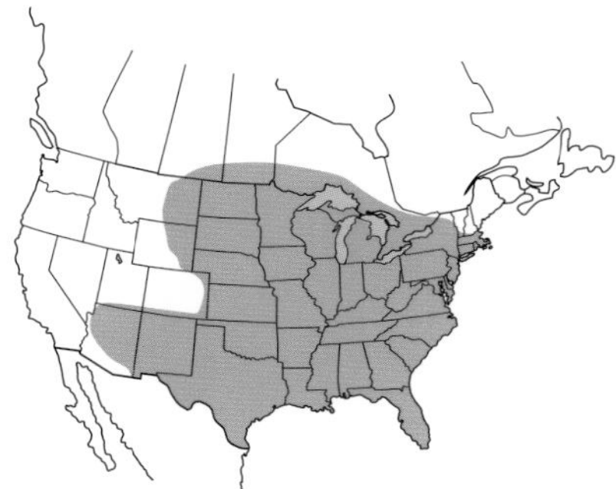

**EXPOSURE**
Sun

**SOIL MOISTURE**
Average to dry to very dry

**BLOOM TIME**
Summer to fall

## COMPANION SPECIES

Other prairie species such as New Jersey tea, lanceleaf tickseed, prairie Junegrass (*Koelaria macrantha*), purple prairie clover (*Dalea purpurea*), few-leaf sunflower (*Helianthus occidentalis*), rough blazing star (*Liatris aspera*), and little bluestem go well with whorled milkweed.

| FLOWER COLOR | HEIGHT | AVAILABILITY |
|---|---|---|
| White | 1 to 3 feet (0.3 to 0.9 m) | Wide |

29.

# Woolly Milkweed

*Asclepias vestita*

This decidedly gray-green broadleaved plant has a sprawling, clumplike growth habit with large flowers that usually remain tucked below the tallest leaves. Although it shares the same savannah and foothill habitat as other California milkweeds, it appears to be less common than they are. It is occasionally available from specialty native plant nurseries and probably is best companion-planted with native bunch grasses to help prop up the short, downward-leaning stems.

| EXPOSURE | SOIL MOISTURE | BLOOM TIME |
|---|---|---|
| Sun | Dry | Late spring, summer |

## USES

Neglected areas/tough sites

Xeriscape

## NATIVE RANGE

| FLOWER COLOR | HEIGHT | AVAILABILITY |
|---|---|---|
| Cream, yellow | 1 to 3 feet (0.3 to 0.9 m) | Limited |

# 30. Woollypod Milkweed

*Asclepias eriocarpa*

Its broad, fuzzy foliage, covered by soft white hairs, and silvery leaf undersides give woollypod milkweed an attractive appearance, especially with a backdrop of other California grassland plants that turn from bright green to golden yellow over the growing season. Woollypod is a plant of hot, rocky hillsides, mountain foothills, and valley grasslands on both sides of the Central Valley. Its upright stems, stature, and leaf shape have much in common with showy milkweed, and indeed the two species can hybridize with each other when planted in close proximity.

| EXPOSURE | SOIL MOISTURE | BLOOM TIME |
|---|---|---|
| Sun | Low | Summer to fall |

Among California milkweeds, this is one of the earlier-emerging species where it occurs near the coast, making it an important host plant for Western monarchs as they move inland in spring, searching for places to lay eggs. High levels of cardenolides also make it a valuable source of chemical protection for the monarchs that feed on it. Although this is a generally upright, free-standing plant, woollypod stems may tend to lean or droop along the ground without support from native grasses.

## USES

**Ornamental**

**Neglected areas/tough sites**

**Xeriscape**

## NATIVE RANGE

## COMPANION SPECIES

Good potential companion species include native grasses such as purple needlegrass (*Nassella pulchra*), California melicgrass (*Melica californica*), prairie Junegrass (*Koeleria macrantha*), and California fescue (*Festuca californica*).

| FLOWER COLOR | HEIGHT | AVAILABILITY |
|---|---|---|
| White, pink | 2 to 4 feet (0.6 to 1.2 m) | Limited |

# 31. Zizotes Milkweed

*Asclepias oenotheroides*

For dry, sandy locations, zizotes is a well-adapted plant with exceptionally long, exposed flower structures. Blooming typically follows periods of rainfall, and the plant persists well even in drought conditions. These factors, along with its short height, make it a useful plant for xeriscaping and where water conservation is a priority. Another of its common names is side-cluster milkweed.

## USES

**Neglected areas/tough sites**

**Xeriscape**

## NATIVE RANGE

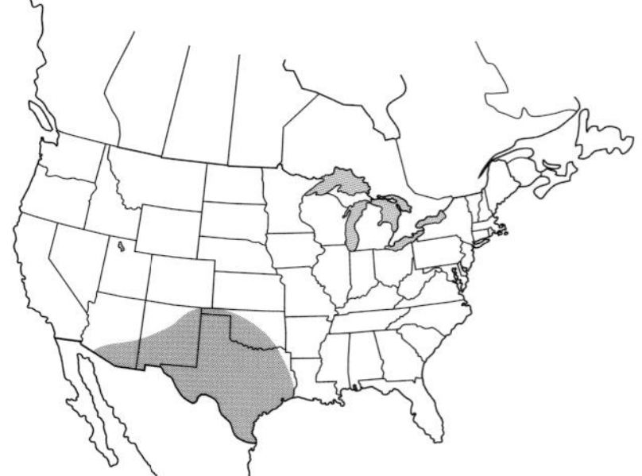

| EXPOSURE | SOIL MOISTURE | BLOOM TIME |
|---|---|---|
| Sun | Dry | Spring to fall |

| FLOWER COLOR | HEIGHT | AVAILABILITY |
|---|---|---|
| Green, purple | 1 to 3 feet (0.3 to 0.9 m) | Limited |

# 4
# Non-Milkweed Host Plants

Three additional genera in the same family as milkweeds—the dogbane family, Apocynaceae—are native to North America and have similar plant chemistry and a host relationship with monarchs. These plants may or may not have milky latex, and the seedpods, seeds, and floss are similar to those of milkweeds. The flowers have five petals, often long and with separation between them so they appear starlike. There is a central column, and pollen is packaged into pollinia (see pages 51–53).

As each common name implies, these are trailing or climbing vines and lack the upright stems of milkweeds.

32.

APOCYNACEAE/ASCLEPIADACEAE

# Honeyvine

*Cynanchum laeve*

Although honeyvine is a native vine in the same family as milkweeds, it belongs to a different genus. Found throughout the central United States from the lower Midwest east to the Atlantic and south to the Gulf states, honeyvine is valuable as a host plant for monarchs, especially since its distribution lies within the heart of the range of the Eastern monarch population.

Honeyvine has three similarities with milkweed: Monarchs use it as a host plant; its fruits are pods (follicles); and its seeds are a flat teardrop

| EXPOSURE | SOIL MOISTURE | BLOOM TIME |
| --- | --- | --- |
| Sun to part shade | Moist to dry | Summer |

shape with attached fluffy coma. Obvious differences from milkweeds are that honeyvine lacks milky latex and has a sprawling or vining growth habit.

The leaves, arranged in opposite pairs along the main stems, are heart-shaped, narrowing to a pointed tip. Honeyvine will grow well on a trellis, with dark, ivylike leaves and many sets of small, white star-shaped flowers. It can also grow too much and require trimming or digging to keep it a desirable size.

The white flowers are excellent nectar sources, attracting butterflies, bees, and other pollinators. Due to its deep roots and vining nature, it has been classified as a noxious weed in Kansas, but no other state considers it as such.

Honeyvine (*C. laeve*) is the most widespread, but there are about 20 *Cynanchum* species native to North America and the Caribbean. Two other species of *Cynanchum* are nonnative, however, and behave as invasive plants: Louise's swallow-wort or black swallow-wort (*C. louiseae*) and European swallow-wort or pale swallow-wort (*C. rossicum*), both originating in southern Europe. (For more on these nonnative honeyvines, see Not All Host Plants Are Good Hosts, page 29.)

## USES

**Ornamental**

**Hedgerow/screen/shade**

### ADDITIONAL HOST PLANT FOR:

Obscure sphinx moth (*Erinnyis obscura*), queen butterfly (*Danaus gilippus*), milkweed tussock moth (*Euchaetes egle*), Florida eucereon moth (*Nelphe carolina*), Florida milkweed vine moth (*Glyphodes floridalis*), faithful beauty moth (*Composia fidelissima*)

## NATIVE RANGE

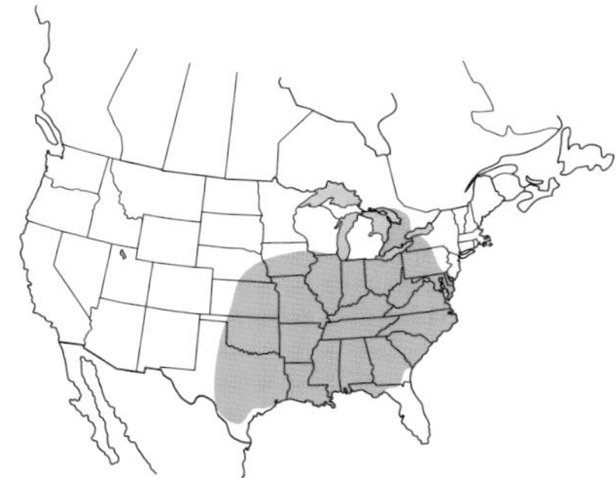

| FLOWER COLOR | HEIGHT | AVAILABILITY |
| --- | --- | --- |
| White | Varies according to support; may sprawl | Limited |

33.

APOCYNACEAE/ASCLEPIADACEAE

# Milkvine

*Matelea* spp.

The natural range for milkvine is from Pennsylvania into the Ohio River valley and Ozarks, throughout the Southeast and Gulf Coast, and along the southern tier of states from Florida to California, near the Mexican border.

Milkvines are weak vines and often trail along the ground in their shaded wooded habitats. The leaves are large and round, with prominent veins and a cleft at the leaf base. The flowers are variable, ranging from simple green to dark burgundy pinwheels of five petals. The fruits look like milkweed fruits,

| EXPOSURE | SOIL MOISTURE | BLOOM TIME |
|---|---|---|
| Sun to part shade | Average, well-drained, rocky | Spring to early summer |

tapered pods with soft spines and the familiar brown seeds with tufts of floss for dispersal in the wind. The stems and leaves have fine hairs.

## RECOMMENDED SPECIES

There are around 25 species of milkvine, but nearly all of these are very rare or quite limited in their natural distribution. As such, they are difficult to find as plants or seeds from nurseries. If you are in the range and habitat for milkvine, ask your local native plant grower if they can produce the plant.

There are two species offered by a few nurseries. One is oldfield milkweed (*M. decipiens*), which grows in the Ozarks of Missouri and Arkansas and also in Louisiana, Oklahoma, and eastern Texas. The other is angular-fruit milkvine (*M. gonocarpos*), whose pod has sharp edges and smooth, flat sides, although it is still a follicle.

Netted milkvine (*M. reticulata*) is used by monarchs in central Texas and the lower Rio Grande valley. Baldwin's milkvine (*M. baldwyniana*) and maroon Carolina milkvine (*M. carolinensis*) are others with garden and ornamental potential as plants for monarchs. When buying plants or seeds, ask the supplier to disclose the origin of the plants, and don't accept plants from producers whose practices endanger rare plants or sensitive populations.

## USES

**Ornamental**

**Hedgerow/screen/shade**

### ADDITIONAL HOST PLANT FOR:

Milkweed tussock moth (*Euchaetes egle*), queen butterfly (*Danaus gilippus*)

## NATIVE RANGE

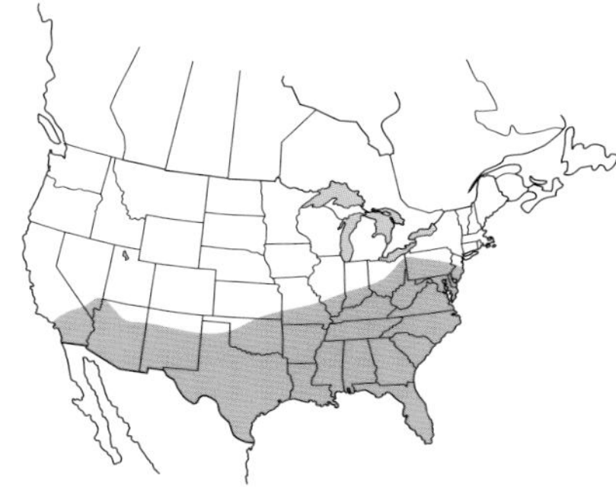

| FLOWER COLOR | HEIGHT | AVAILABILITY |
| --- | --- | --- |
| Purple-brown, burgundy, green, white (depending on species) | 3 to 6 feet (0.9 to 1.8 m); can climb higher if supported | Limited |

# 34.

APOCYNACEAE/ASCLEPIADACEAE

# Twinevine

## *Funastrum* spp.

The third native vine that is a host plant for monarchs is twinevine, a southern species with a native distribution from the Southwest through Texas, Oklahoma, and along the Gulf Coast, to Florida and the southern Atlantic coast. Fringed twinevine (*F. cynanchoides*) is an excellent choice for the Desert Southwest including inland California. The plants have milky latex, narrow leaves, and a vining habit. The flowers are gorgeous; each lobe is fringed with hairs.

### USES

**Ornamental**

**Neglected areas/tough sites**

**Xeriscape**

### ADDITIONAL HOST PLANT FOR:

Soldier butterfly (*Danaus eresimus*), queen butterfly (*Danaus gilippus*), obscure sphinx moth (*Erinnyis obscura*), Florida eucereon (*Nelphe carolina*)

### NATIVE RANGE

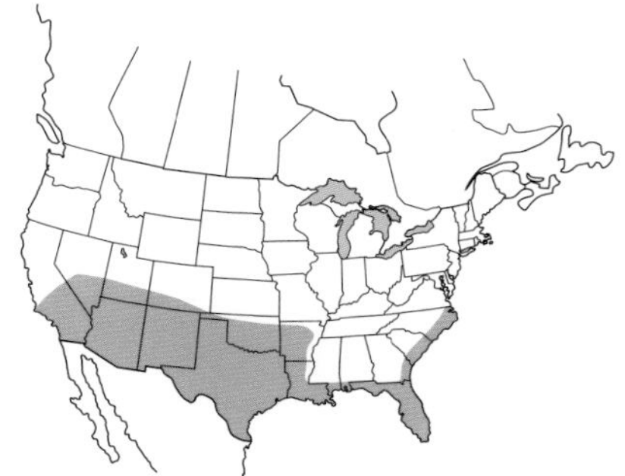

| EXPOSURE | SOIL MOISTURE | BLOOM TIME |
| --- | --- | --- |
| Sun | Dry | Spring and summer |

| FLOWER COLOR | HEIGHT | AVAILABILITY |
| --- | --- | --- |
| Pale to dark pink with white | Varies with support | Limited |

# 5

# Nectar Plants: Native Wildflowers

Nectar plants are the key to attracting monarchs throughout the growing season, whether they are laying eggs or migrating. The best butterfly habitats are those that provide flowering plants from spring into fall.

For monarchs, fall-blooming plants such as goldenrods and asters are especially important, fueling the journey to overwintering sites and the long rest period ahead. Conversely, early-blooming plants such as penstemons provide a much-needed spring jolt of sugary energy as monarchs seek out newly emerging milkweeds. By providing a succession of flowers, you'll not only support monarchs but you're guaranteed visits by other butterflies as well.

# 35.

## ASTERACEAE

# Aster

## *Aster* spp., *Symphyotrichum* spp.

Slightly fewer than 100 aster species are found across North America, with at least one occurring everywhere within the monarch's range in the United States and Canada. Given this vast diversity, most gardeners can find at least one species that will work for their local conditions. These generally fall-blooming plants can vary significantly in color, height, and tolerance for shade and soil moisture, so it is worth doing some research to identify optimal local species for your situation.

As a general rule, asters reach their full flowering potential in rich soils with good organic matter, although there are exceptions. A few species, such as New England aster (*S. novae-angliae*), can get extremely tall and lanky. They may flop over when grown in gardens without the benefit of strong competition and support from other wild plants around them. Cutting back these asters to around 12 inches (31 cm) in height in early summer encourages a shorter, bushy plant that also tends to produce more flowers.

Like goldenrod, these plants are extremely valuable for providing late-season nectar to fall-migrating butterflies.

| EXPOSURE | SOIL MOISTURE | BLOOM TIME |
| --- | --- | --- |
| Sun to part shade | Medium to wet | Fall |

| FLOWER COLOR | HEIGHT | AVAILABILITY |
|---|---|---|
| White, purple, pink, blue | 1 to 5 feet (0.3 to 1.5 m) | Wide |

## RECOMMENDED SPECIES

An entire book could be devoted to North American asters and still just scratch the surface of their ecology. Look for the species native to your region with the largest flowers, to maximize monarch nectar value. Some of the species we use in restoration work include Pacific aster (*S. chilense*) on the West Coast; Eaton's aster (*S. eatonii*) for the inland west (including inland British Columbia and the prairie provinces south all the way to Arizona and New Mexico); and smooth blue aster (*S. laeve*) for the Rocky Mountains and upper Midwest.

Calico aster (*S. lateriflorum*) and white arrowleaf aster (*S. urophyllum*), both of which have some shade tolerance, attract impressive numbers of insects and occur across nearly all of eastern North America. New England aster (*S. novae-angliae*) and New York aster (*S. novi-belgii*) are most common in the Northeast and Great Lakes regions, where with goldenrod they sometimes form wonderfully colorful autumn thickets in newly cleared forest edges.

## USES

**Ornamental**

**Containers**

**Wildflower meadow/prairie restoration**

**Rain garden/wetland**

## ADDITIONAL HOST PLANT FOR:

Common buckeye butterfly (*Junonia coenia*), pearl crescent butterfly (*Phyciodes tharos*), aster borer moth (*Papaipema impecuniosa*), Northern checkerspot butterfly (*Chlosyne palla*)

## NATIVE RANGE

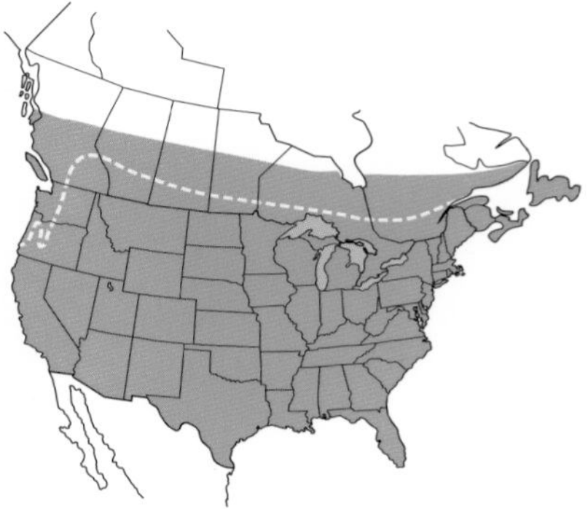

# 36.

## LAMIACEAE

# Beebalm, Wild Bergamot

### *Monarda* spp.

These native members of the mint family are excellent pollinator plants with very different flower sizes and shapes. The *Monarda* genus includes plants that, depending on the species, may attract some pollinator groups (such as hummingbirds or small native bees, for example) more than others. That said, their showy appearance and very adaptable nature make all of them interesting and useful in native plant gardens. Moreover, as a group, most beebalm species establish very reliably from seed, adding to their value in large meadow-type plantings where the cost of transplants would be prohibitive.

| EXPOSURE | SOIL MOISTURE | BLOOM TIME |
|---|---|---|
| Sun to part shade | Medium to dry | Summer |

In addition to monarchs, the spectacular beebalms attract other showy butterflies, dramatic hawk moths, bumblebees, and hummingbirds.

## RECOMMENDED SPECIES

The eighteen beebalm species in North America occur from southeastern Canada south to Florida and west to the Rocky Mountains, and they include both annuals and perennials. Many are uncommon or occur only in a few limited areas of the Southwest. The most widely available and reliable monarch plant is the lavender-flowered common wild bergamot (*M. fistulosa*), which is adaptable across most of the United States and southern Canada. The similar-looking (but red-flowered) Oswego tea (*M. didyma*) has a smaller native range, spanning the eastern Great Lakes region and Appalachia; it is another excellent monarch plant and highly ornamental. Both prefer fertile, slightly damp soil and partial to full sun.

## USES

**Ornamental**

**Wildflower meadow/prairie restoration**

## NATIVE RANGE

## ADDITIONAL HOST PLANT FOR:

Hermit sphinx moth (*Lintneria eremitus*)

| FLOWER COLOR | HEIGHT | AVAILABILITY |
|---|---|---|
| Lavender, red, purple, white, pink | 1 to 4 feet (0.3 to 1.2 m) | Wide |

37.

ASTERACEAE

# Beggarticks

*Bidens* spp.

Consisting primarily of wetland or marsh species, beggarticks usually tolerate mucky soils and occasional flooding. Although they are ignored even by native plant gardeners, and deplored for their sharp two-pronged seeds that stick to clothing, this group of annual and biennial species has long been recognized by duck hunters and wetland conservationists as an important food plant for waterfowl and wetland songbirds. In fact, some speculate that beggarticks can colonize new wetlands by embedding themselves into the feathers of ducks, resulting in nearly nationwide distribution of some species.

| EXPOSURE | SOIL MOISTURE | BLOOM TIME |
|---|---|---|
| Sun to part shade | Wet to average | Late summer |

The *Bidens* genus is divided into two broad groups: those species with ray flowers that resemble simple sunflower- or *Coreopsis*-like blossoms, and the species with only a tight cluster of central disk flowers (resembling a small sunflower without the outer ring of petals). Both groups have slender, pointed compound leaves on branching stems and foliage that may turn purple in late-season cool weather. Many species lack any floral scent, yet they are all typically very attractive to numerous species of flower visitors, including solitary bees, moths, and butterflies.

Beggarticks are underutilized in native plant restoration, where they are excellent for rain gardens, roadside ditches, stormwater management ponds, and other tough sites prone to inundation. Note, however, that because they are mostly annual species, they will decline in abundance without occasional disturbance to clear away competing vegetation and create bare ground for the plants to reseed themselves. In some planting locations, seasonal flooding alone may create enough vacant spaces for this to occur.

## USES

**Wildflower meadow/prairie restoration**

**Neglected areas/tough sites**

**Rain garden/wetland/stormwater management**

## ADDITIONAL HOST PLANT FOR:

Bidens borer moth (*Epiblema otiosana*)

## NATIVE RANGE

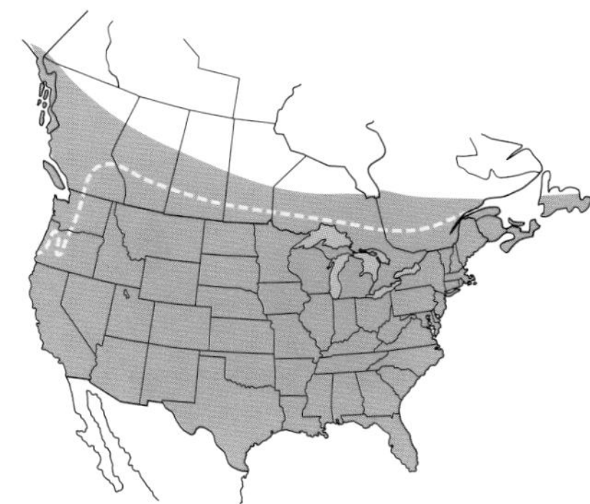

| FLOWER COLOR | HEIGHT | AVAILABILITY |
| --- | --- | --- |
| Yellow | 4 to 5 feet (1.2 to 1.5 m) | Variable by region |

## RECOMMENDED SPECIES

A dozen species of beggarticks are distributed across North America, including some uncommon ones; nevertheless, the plants tend to have limited commercial availability. Specialty seed nurseries that focus on wetland restoration are the best places to track down commercially available sources of these plants.

Note that common names for this genus tend to be inconsistent and subject to regional variation, but some of the more common species to watch for include tickseed sunflower (*B. aristosa*), which occurs in the central Midwest and south to the Mississippi Delta region; Spanish needles (*B. bipinnata*), found in the Mid-Atlantic states, the central Midwest, and the Southwest (Arizona and New Mexico); and three species found almost nationwide but most abundantly in northern states—nodding beggartick (*B. cernua*), devil's beggartick (*B. frondosa*), and big devil's beggartick (*B. vulgata*).

38.

ASTERACEAE

# Blanketflower

*Gaillardia* spp.

These brightly colored annual and perennial wildflowers are both drought tolerant and long blooming, attracting monarch butterflies, Northwestern fritillaries (*Speyeria hesperis*), orange sulphurs (*Colias eurytheme*), and many native bees. Annual species tend to be easier to establish from seed than perennial species.

| EXPOSURE | SOIL MOISTURE | BLOOM TIME |
|---|---|---|
| Sun | Average to dry | Summer |

## RECOMMENDED SPECIES

Nearly a dozen species of blanketflower are found in North America, but only two are widely available as seed or garden plants. Blanketflower (*G. aristata*) is a perennial species of the northern plains, Rocky Mountains, and the inland Northwest. Indian blanket (*G. pulchella*) is an annual species occurring from Arizona across the southern plains, Gulf Coast, and Florida.

## USES

**Ornamental**

**Container**

**Wildflower meadow/prairie restoration**

**Neglected areas/tough sites**

## NATIVE RANGE

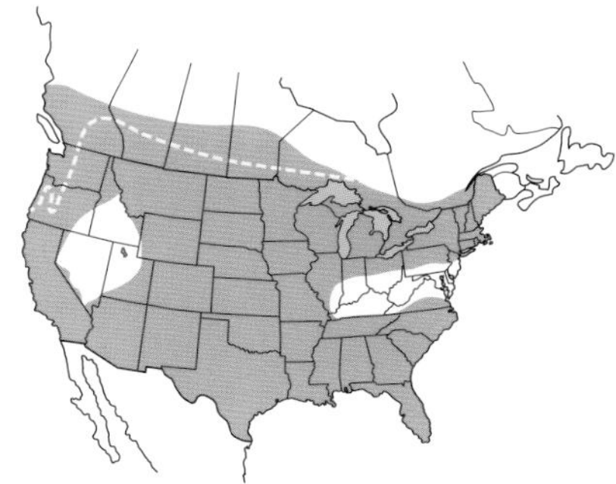

## ADDITIONAL HOST PLANT FOR:

Blanketflower moth (*Schinia masoni*), bordered patch butterfly (*Chlosyne lacinia*), sunflower moth (*Homoeosoma electella*), bina flower moth (*Schinia bina*)

| FLOWER COLOR | HEIGHT | AVAILABILITY |
|---|---|---|
| Orange, yellow | 2 feet (0.6 m) | Wide |

39.

ASTERACEAE

# Blazing Star

*Liatris* spp.

Among the most effective and reliable monarch butterfly magnets, blazing stars deserve special attention. Some species, meadow blazing star (*L. ligulistylis*) in particular, have incredible drawing power, most likely offering windborne chemical cues to attract butterflies.

In fact, meadow blazing star is known for seeming to attract monarchs from long distances. Although all *Liatris* are excellent monarch plants, the authors have seen large numbers of monarchs bypass huge fields of towering prairie blazing star (*L. pycnostachya*) to seek out a few small and

| EXPOSURE | SOIL MOISTURE | BLOOM TIME |
|---|---|---|
| Sun to part shade | Medium | Summer |

insignificant meadow blazing stars. In a garden they provide overlapping and extended bloom, maximizing nectar availability.

This diverse and widespread group of wildflowers grow from tuberlike corms and bloom for a long period, opening first at the top of the flower spike and sequentially opening lower flowers over many weeks. They are must-have plants for any monarch garden east of the Rocky Mountains.

## RECOMMENDED SPECIES

Forty-eight species of blazing stars are found from southern Quebec and Ontario south to Florida and west to the Rocky Mountains. Several of these are not widespread or common. As a group they are all beautiful and structurally interesting plants, though, and many species have become commercially available, including meadow blazing star (*L. ligulistylis*, found in the upper Midwest and Great Plains). Prairie blazing star (*L. pycnostachya*) and the much smaller cylindrical blazing star (*L. cylindricea*) may occur along the entire length of the Mississippi River valley. Marsh blazing star (*L. spicata*) is native to the eastern United States from New England to Florida, and rough blazing star (*L. aspera*) is most common in the Great Plains.

## USES

**Ornamental**

**Wildflower meadow/prairie restoration**

**Rain garden/wetland**

### ADDITIONAL HOST PLANT FOR:

Wavy-lined emerald moth (*Synchlora aerata*), blazing star borer moth (*Carmenta anthracipennis*), blazing star borer moth (*Papaipema beeriana*)

## NATIVE RANGE

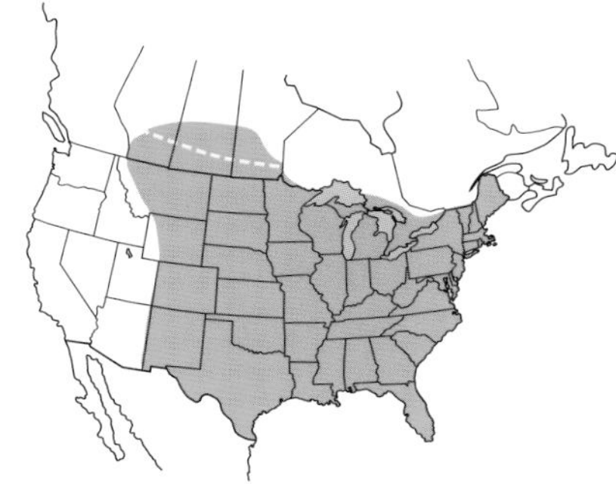

| FLOWER COLOR | HEIGHT | AVAILABILITY |
|---|---|---|
| Lavender | 1 to 6 feet (0.3 to 1.8 m) | Wide |

# 40.

LILIACEAE

# Blue Dicks, Snakelily

*Dichelostemma* spp.

Western, lilylike plants in the asparagus family, blue dicks are perennials that resprout from an underground bulb (corm) each season. The flowers are shades of blue-purple, radiating out in an umbel, and are quite showy, even if the individual plants are not large. Once securely established in a garden, blue dicks can be propagated by dividing the corms and planting in new areas.

| EXPOSURE | SOIL MOISTURE | BLOOM TIME |
| --- | --- | --- |
| Sun to part shade | Average to dry | Late winter, early spring |

## RECOMMENDED SPECIES

Blue dicks (*D. capitatum*) is used by monarchs and grows through much of California and other western states. The underground corms survive moderate wildfire; the plant is often conspicuous in blooming after fires, before other vegetation has regrown and while more sun reaches the plants below the canopy.

## USES

**Ornamental**

**Wildflower meadow/prairie restoration**

**Neglected areas/tough sites**

## NATIVE RANGE

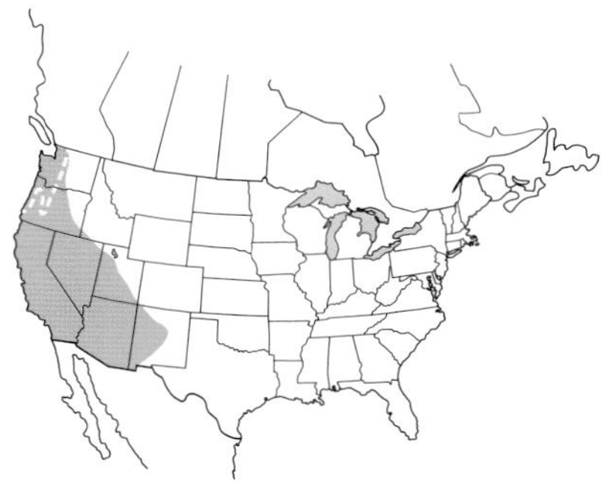

## ADDITIONAL HOST PLANT FOR:

The use of blue dicks as a host plant by other moths or butterflies has not been observed.

| FLOWER COLOR | HEIGHT | AVAILABILITY |
|---|---|---|
| Purple, blue, pink | 1 to 3 feet (0.3 to 0.9 m) | Variable by region |

# 41.

## ASTERACEAE

# Boneset, Joe Pye Weed

## *Eupatorium* spp., *Eutrochium* spp.

These two groups of plants were long lumped together by taxonomists but recently have been separated into different groups. Despite the taxonomic reshuffling, they remain close relatives and share a number of ecological traits.

Boneset's big clusters of small white flowers are popular with many types of insects besides monarchs, including other showy butterflies such as various species of swallowtails. These handsome plants never seem to appear far from wetlands, damp ditches, and very fertile soils—yet when transplanted and cared for, they can survive and even thrive in many typical front-yard prairies and well-tended butterfly gardens.

Like milkweeds, boneset plants have a complex (and mostly poisonous) chemistry that attracts a group of specialist herbivores adapted to these chemicals, including the ruby tiger moth (*Phragmatobia fuliginosa*), the three-lined flower moth (*Schinia trifascia*), the boneset borer moth (*Carmenta pyralidiformis*), and the clymene moth (*Haploa clymene*). Historically, the complex chemistry of these species led to a belief in their homeopathic medicinal value as bone-setting plants, giving them their common name.

Like boneset, the joe pye weeds are also top plants for attracting a striking diversity of other butterflies, as well as bumblebees, leafcutter bees, and many smaller flower visitors. In an optimal location, the large, pink, showy flower clusters on these plants can tower high above the average person's head. Prime spots have rich, fertile, damp soils and are slightly shaded during part of the day, such as, for example, the edges of forests.

Joe pye weeds are great for gardens under a few overhead shade trees, and they make dramatic and interesting plants when located near downspouts and other damp areas.

| EXPOSURE | SOIL MOISTURE | BLOOM TIME |
| --- | --- | --- |
| Sun to part shade | Medium to wet | Summer |

Joe pye weed thrives in damp, rich soils and even tolerates partial shade. Once established, these towering plants can live for decades.

| FLOWER COLOR | HEIGHT | AVAILABILITY |
|---|---|---|
| Pink, white | 1 to 8 feet (0.3 to 2.4 m) | Variable by region |

## RECOMMENDED SPECIES

Depending on the classification system, there are roughly 30 species of boneset plants, mostly occurring from Maine to Florida and extending west across southern Canada and into the central United States. Of these various plants, however, common boneset (*Eupatorium perfoliatum*) is the most widespread, appreciated, and commercially available (several others are weeds).

All five species of joe pye weed are limited to the eastern United States and Canada. Three of the most widespread are spotted joe pye weed (*Eutrochium maculatum*), hollow joe pye weed (*E. fistulosum*), and sweet-scented joe pye weed (*E. purpureum*).

---

## USES

**Ornamental**

**Wildflower meadow/ prairie restoration**

**Rain garden/wetland**

## ADDITIONAL HOST PLANTS FOR:

Ruby tiger moth (*Phragmatobia fuliginosa*), eupatorium borer moth (*Carmenta bassiformis*), eupatorium plume moth (*Oidaematophorus eupatorii*), Virginia tiger moth or yellow woolybear moth (*Spilosoma virginica*)

## NATIVE RANGE

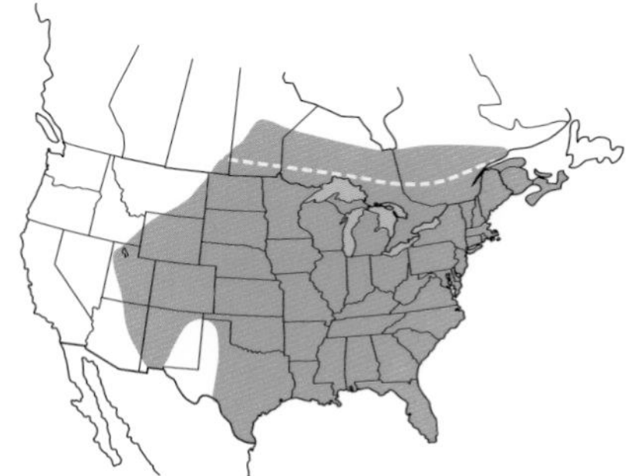

Once established in favorable conditions over several years, boneset develops into a dense, shrublike, multistemmed plant with masses of blooms.

42.

ASTERACEAE

# Brickellbush, False Boneset

*Brickellia* spp.

With dozens of species native to North America, this is a large genus. As nectar plants, *Brickellia* offer hundreds of heads of dusty white flowers with disk florets in late summer.

Brickellbush are host plants for several noctuid moths in the genus *Schinia*. The leaves are deep green or gray-green and vary in shape from arrow-shaped to very narrow.

| EXPOSURE | SOIL MOISTURE | BLOOM TIME |
|---|---|---|
| Sun, light shade | Average to dry | Late summer, fall |

## RECOMMENDED SPECIES

False boneset (*B. eupatorioides*) is a perennial with a native range across most of the United States except the extreme west. California brickellbush (*B. californica*) is a complementary western species and is a small shrub. The flowers are not showy, but the fragrance of the nectar adds to this plant's appeal in gardens. Both are available through a modest number of native plant nurseries.

## USES

**Wildflower meadow/prairie restoration**

**Neglected areas/tough sites**

## ADDITIONAL HOST PLANT FOR:

*Richia grotei*, slender flower moth (*Schinia gracilenta*), and *Schinia oleagina*

## NATIVE RANGE

| FLOWER COLOR | HEIGHT | AVAILABILITY |
|---|---|---|
| White, cream | 3 to 5 feet (0.9 to 1.5 m) | Variable by region |

43.

FABACEAE

# Clover

*Trifolium* spp.

A common sight in pastures, hayfields, old fields, roadsides, and lawns, clover is a familiar plant to many. You may also recognize it from artistic depictions in photographs and paintings, often with a butterfly or bee nectaring on the flower. Clover flowers are rich in nectar, and, as legumes, their roots host beneficial bacteria that capture and release nitrogen in the soil, enriching its fertility for neighboring plants. The rounded clover flower clusters are made up of dozens of diminutive individual flowers, each with the classic "pea" or papilionoid (which actually means "butterfly-like") shape.

| EXPOSURE | SOIL MOISTURE | BLOOM TIME |
| --- | --- | --- |
| Sun | Moist to dry | Spring, summer |

## RECOMMENDED SPECIES

Red clover (*T. pratense*) and white clover (*T. repens*) are of European origin but, like all clovers, are excellent nectar plants. They are widely naturalized and sown as forages or cover crops, and when managed for flowering they are excellent food sources for bees and butterflies. The flowers of white clover are very low to the ground and often persist in lawns, making the turf more bee friendly.

There is more diversity beyond red and white clovers. In North America, the native species of *Trifolium* are primarily western species. Annuals are foothill clover (*T. ciliolatum*), tomcat clover (*T. willdenovii*), bull clover (*T. fucatum*), and clammy clover (*T. obtusiflorum*); cows clover (*T. wormskioldii*) is perennial. There are native clovers in the eastern states, but many are considered rare, threatened, or endangered.

## USES

**Wildflower meadow/prairie restoration**

**Neglected areas/tough sites**

**Xeriscape**

## NATIVE RANGE

## ADDITIONAL HOST PLANT FOR:

Greenish blue butterfly (*Plebejus saepiolus*), Eastern tailed-blue butterfly (*Cupido comyntas*), Western cloudywing butterfly (*Thorybes diversus*), clouded sulphur butterfly (*Colias philodice*), Southern cloudywing (*Thorybes bathyllus*)

| FLOWER COLOR | HEIGHT | AVAILABILITY |
| --- | --- | --- |
| White, pink, yellow, red, purple | 2 to 24 inches (5 to 61 cm) | Variable by region |

44.

ASTERACEAE

# Coneflower, Black-eyed Susan

*Rudbeckia* spp.

The most common member of this genus, the black-eyed Susan (*R. hirta*), is typically a poor monarch plant, providing only small amounts of nectar; however, it is prolific, easy to grow, and widespread. All of these traits make it a decent resource, supporting butterflies with its sheer abundance and hardiness. Black-eyed Susan also grows quickly, often flowering the first year after seeding. As a result it is a useful visual marker for new prairie

| EXPOSURE | SOIL MOISTURE | BLOOM TIME |
|---|---|---|
| Sun | Medium | Summer |

plantings, helping neighbors understand that you're not simply letting the front yard turn into a weedy mess! Moreover, the long-lasting flowers of this humble plant are excellent at bridging the bloom times of earlier- and later-flowering species, ensuring some availability of nectar through long stretches of the growing season.

All that said, other species in this genus are probably more valuable and sought out by monarchs and other pollinators. And fortunately there are several other great species with which to supplement butterfly gardens.

## USES

**Ornamental**

**Containers**

**Wildflower meadow/prairie restoration**

**Neglected areas/tough sites**

**Rain garden/wetland**

## NATIVE RANGE

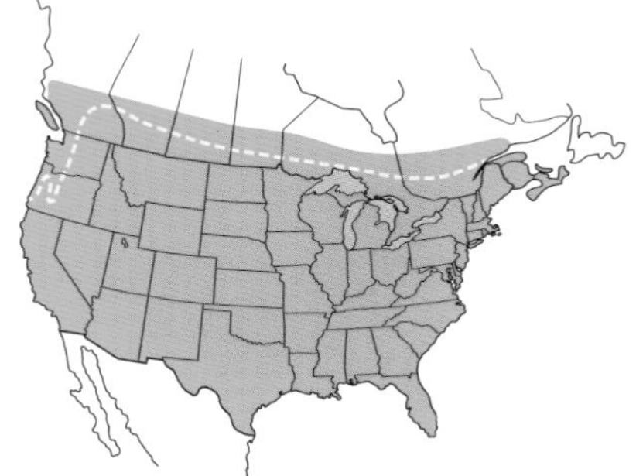

## ADDITIONAL HOST PLANT FOR:

Coneflower borer moth (*Papaipema nelita*), silvery checkerspot butterfly (*Chlosyne nycteis*)

| FLOWER COLOR | HEIGHT | AVAILABILITY |
| --- | --- | --- |
| Yellow, brown | 1 to 6 feet (0.3 to 1.8 m) | Wide |

## RECOMMENDED SPECIES

Avoid ornamental varieties of *Rudbeckia* for butterfly gardens, since wild-type plants tend to be most attractive to insects. In addition to black-eyed Susan, which is found across nearly all of southeastern Canada and the eastern United States, cutleaf coneflower (*R. laciniata*) is an excellent butterfly (and bee!) plant for wetter soils.

In the Mississippi and Ohio River valleys, brown-eyed Susan (*R. triloba*) is a short-lived species that reseeds itself and tends to hum with small insects and occasional larger ones, monarchs included. In the West, the striking western coneflower (*R. occidentalis*) tends to occur at higher elevations and in damp locations. It has no petals; instead the central cluster of brown disk flowers simply rises atop thick green stems, giving it an otherworldly scepterlike appearance and the occasionally used common name "green wizard."

# 45.

LAMIACEAE

## Coyote Mint

*Monardella* spp.

Western species that grow well in dry or rocky soils, coyote mints provide colorful, nectar-rich flowers. In the wild they are found in chaparral, coastal scrub, and other wooded sites. Like most mints, these are great nectar plants for butterflies and bees.

| EXPOSURE | SOIL MOISTURE | BLOOM TIME |
| --- | --- | --- |
| Sun | Dry | Summer |

## RECOMMENDED SPECIES

Coyote mint (*M. villosa*) is a slightly woody perennial with pops of purple flowers held high above gray-green opposite leaves. Mountain monardella (*M. odorotissima*) is low growing and forms dense mats of aromatic leaves with splashy clusters of purple blooms.

## USES

**Ornamental**

**Wildflower meadow/prairie restoration**

**Neglected areas/tough sites**

**Xeriscape**

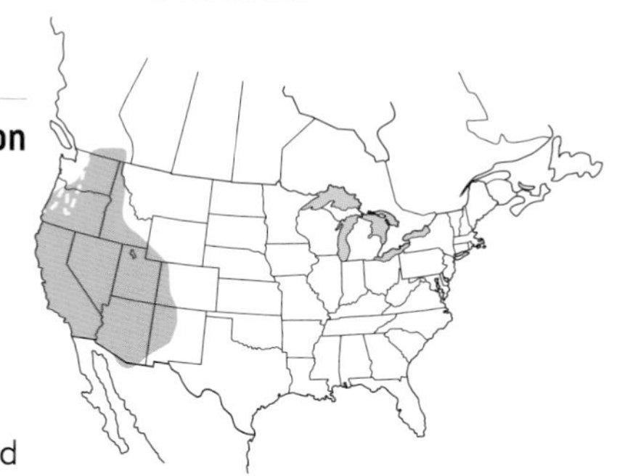

## ADDITIONAL HOST PLANT FOR:

Several species of *Pyrausta* moths and hermit sphinx moth (*Lintneria eremitus*)

| FLOWER COLOR | HEIGHT | AVAILABILITY |
| --- | --- | --- |
| Purple, pink | 6 to 24 inches (15 to 61 cm) | Wide |

46.

SCROPHULARIACEAE / PLANTAGINACEAE

# Culver's Root

*Veronicastrum* spp.

A prairie plant, Culver's root blooms intensely in midsummer. The flowers are small and white, arranged on candelabra-like spikes. The flowers are very attractive to monarch butterflies and to many native bee species. The elegant foliage appears as whorls of finely toothed dark green leaves along the stems. Tiny seeds form in dark capsules, and the branched candelabra shapes stay upright into the fall and winter. There is a single species of Culver's root in North America: *V. virginicum.*

| EXPOSURE | SOIL MOISTURE | BLOOM TIME |
|---|---|---|
| Sun | Average to wet | Summer |

## USES

**Ornamental**

**Wildflower meadow/prairie restoration**

**Rain garden/wetland/stormwater management**

## ADDITIONAL HOST PLANT FOR:

Culver's root borer moth (*Papaipema sciata*)

## NATIVE RANGE

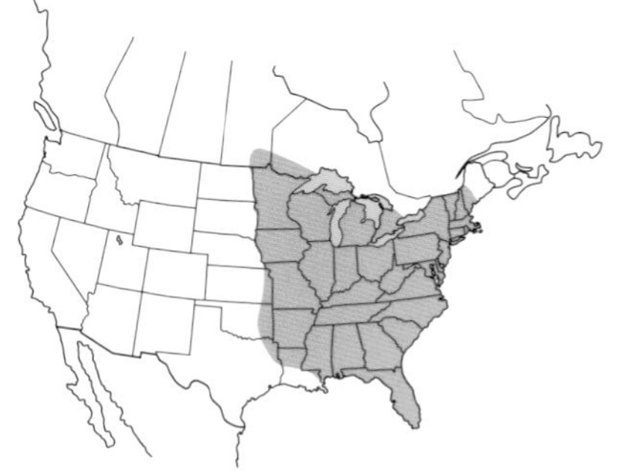

| FLOWER COLOR | HEIGHT | AVAILABILITY |
|---|---|---|
| White | 3 to 6 feet (0.9 to 1.8 m) | Wide |

# 47.

## APOCYNACEAE

# Dogbane

## *Apocynum* spp.

As a close relative to milkweed, this genus has occasionally caused confusion about whether or not monarch caterpillars feed on the foliage of its three North American species. In fact, there is little substantiated evidence of monarchs using dogbane as a caterpillar host plant. Other milkweed specialist insects, however, including the red milkweed beetle, the large milkweed bug, and milkweed aphids, have been observed on these plants that resemble milkweed.

Even though they may not serve as a caterpillar host, the dogbane species are all remarkable plants for the sheer diversity of insects, including monarch butterflies, that are attracted to the flowers for nectar. Some of those common flower-visiting companions are many species of solitary native bees, numerous types of beneficial predatory wasps, various flies, and many other species of butterflies. In previous work by Xerces ecologists, dogbane has been included in seed mixes for planting on farms to attract beneficial insects for natural pest control.

These tough-stemmed, broad-leaved plants produce a milky latex sap just as milkweeds do and can be mistaken for them when sending up new shoots early in the year. Even the white or pink flowers resemble milkweed blooms at a quick glance, but upon close observation the flowers are usually sparser on dogbane, smaller in size, fewer in number, and lacking the characteristic hoods and horns of milkweeds.

Surprisingly, despite their excellent value as insect nectar plants, dogbanes are not widely available, even from native plant nurseries. They typically occur in damp or poorly drained locations, and often in areas with a

| EXPOSURE | SOIL MOISTURE | BLOOM TIME |
|---|---|---|
| Sun to partial shade | Wet to average | Summer |

| FLOWER COLOR | HEIGHT | AVAILABILITY |
| --- | --- | --- |
| White, pink | 4 feet (1.2 m) | Limited |

history of abuse or neglect such as roadside ditches, vacant lots, old railroad lines, wetland edges, and similar sites. With care, dogbane can be successfully started from wild-collected seed, or even from transplanted rhizomes from mature colonies of the plant that often form wherever it is found.

## RECOMMENDED SPECIES

Cultivated varieties of dogbane do not exist, but three species of the genus are found from coast to coast, from Mexico to Southern Canada. *Apocynum androsaemifolium* is slightly more common in the West, while *A. cannabinum* is found across North America and is the more common species in the southeastern United States. At various locations nationwide, a naturally occurring hybrid of the two previously mentioned species can also be found, *A.* × *floribundum*. All three are similar in their preferred habitat, and all are excellent nectar plants for monarchs.

## USES

**Wildflower meadow/prairie restoration**

**Neglected areas/tough sites**

**Rain garden/wetland/stormwater management**

## ADDITIONAL HOST PLANT FOR:

Snowberry clearwing moth (*Hemaris diffinis*)

## NATIVE RANGE

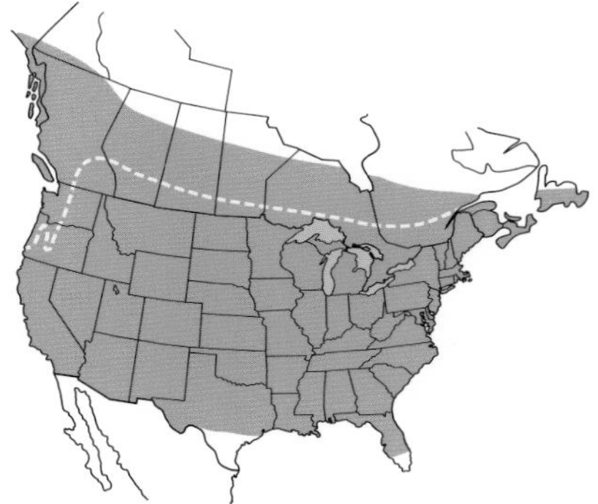

48.

ONAGRACEAE

# Fireweed

*Chamerion angustifolium*

Its name arose from the fact that fireweed is often one of the first plants to extensively colonize previously forested lands after large wildfires. This usually occurs not in the first year after a fire but two or three years later, when tall magenta spikes rise from seeds long dormant below the ashes. They go on to produce their own crop of tiny, fluffy seeds that float on air currents across the western states and the boreal forests of Canada, the Great Lakes, and northern New England.

| EXPOSURE | SOIL MOISTURE | BLOOM TIME |
|---|---|---|
| Sun | Medium | Summer |

As a garden plant, fireweed is incredibly forgiving and requires little special care. It is prone to spreading, however, forming large colonies from a network of rhizomes. Despite this, fireweed is easy to cut back and maintain in a given spot. Moreover, its rhizomes can easily be dug up and transplanted to spread around or to share with gardening friends.

This species is an excellent choice for a tall backdrop behind lower-growing foreground species in a garden. Although it is sometimes browsed by deer and rabbits, fireweed is not a favorite of herbivores. The nectar of this plant is valued by monarchs, and it is also famous among beekeepers for producing extremely high-quality honey.

## RECOMMENDED SPECIES

Fireweed is found from Maine to California and in high elevations across the Southwest. As a cold-climate species, it is mostly absent in the Southeast. A few cultivated varieties are occasionally advertised, and at least one white-flowered fireweed subspecies is sometimes observed in parts of Canada, but these variants are neither common nor are they known to be any better or worse as a butterfly plant. At higher elevations, the similar species dwarf fireweed (*C. latifolium*) can be widespread, but typically it is not available as a nursery plant.

## USES

**Ornamental**

**Neglected areas/tough sites**

**Hedgerow/screen/shade**

## ADDITIONAL HOST PLANT FOR:

Black-banded carpet moth (*Antepirrhoe semiatrata*)

## NATIVE RANGE

| FLOWER COLOR | HEIGHT | AVAILABILITY |
|---|---|---|
| Pink | 2 to 7 feet (0.6 to 2.1 m) | Limited; variable by region |

# 49.

LAMIACEAE

# Giant Hyssop

*Agastache* spp.

Native plants in the genus *Agastache* provide high-sugar nectar for monarch butterflies and many native bees and other pollinators. These annuals or perennials are easy to grow from seed and can fill in garden beds with flowers in shades of purple to white, arranged in a spike at the end of the stems. Members of the mint family, these plants have the characteristic square stem with pairs of opposite leaves.

| EXPOSURE | SOIL MOISTURE | BLOOM TIME |
|---|---|---|
| Sun to part shade | Average | Summer |

The leaves of giant hyssop have an anise or licorice scent when rubbed and can be dried and steeped as an herbal tea. Giant hyssop also makes good cut flowers. A monarch might visit your bouquet on a patio table!

## RECOMMENDED SPECIES

There are several choices for giant hyssop: blue giant hyssop (*A. foeniculum*), purple giant hyssop (*A. scrophulariifolia*), yellow giant hyssop (*A. nepetoides*), and nettle-leaf giant hyssop (*A. urticifolia*).

## USES

**Ornamental**

**Containers**

**Wildflower meadow/prairie restoration**

## ADDITIONAL HOST PLANT FOR:

Northern azure butterfly (*Celastrina lucia*), summer azure butterfly (*Celastrina neglecta*)

## NATIVE RANGE

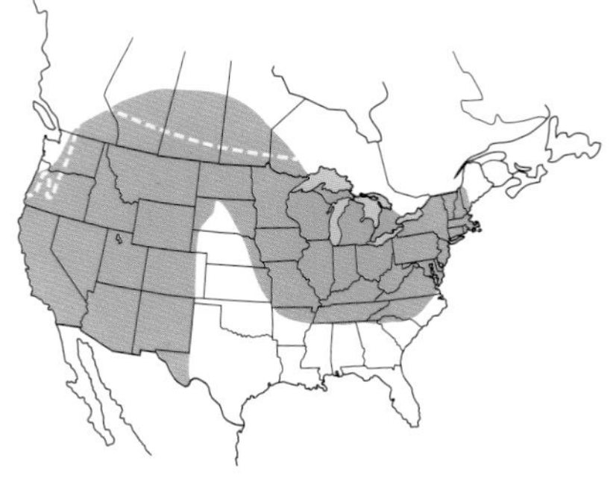

| FLOWER COLOR | HEIGHT | AVAILABILITY |
|---|---|---|
| Purple, white, yellow | 1.5 to 6 feet (0.5 to 1.8 m) | Wide |

50.

MALVACEAE

# Globemallow

*Sphaeralcea* spp.

Plants of the arid inland West, the globemallows range from the dry interior of southern British Columbia all the way south into Mexico. These annual and perennial species with woolly green-gray foliage occupy roadsides, disturbed areas, and scrub deserts, often with creosote bush and sagebrush. In some of these locations, the plants will stay semidormant as miniature scruffy shrubs or dormant seeds, only to come alive after a major rain event, when they spring up from the ground to form carpets of bloom.

| EXPOSURE | SOIL MOISTURE | BLOOM TIME |
|---|---|---|
| Sun | Dry | Spring to summer |

Along with various species of rabbitbrush, desert milkweeds, and brittlebushes, globemallows are ideal for dry landscape gardening. Roughly 30 species of globemallows occur in the United States (and just two or three in Canada), many only in remote areas of Utah, Nevada, and New Mexico.

## RECOMMENDED SPECIES

Scarlet globemallow (*S. coccinea*) is widespread and adaptable, found in the eastern Great Plains west into Nevada and Oregon, and from the prairie provinces of Canada south to Mexico. Also widespread are currantleaf globemallow (*S. grossulariifolia*) and Munro's globemallow (*S. munroana*), found in the Great Basin, the inland Pacific Northwest, and parts of California.

## USES

**Ornamental**

**Wildflower meadow/prairie restoration**

**Neglected areas/tough sites**

**Xeriscape**

## NATIVE RANGE

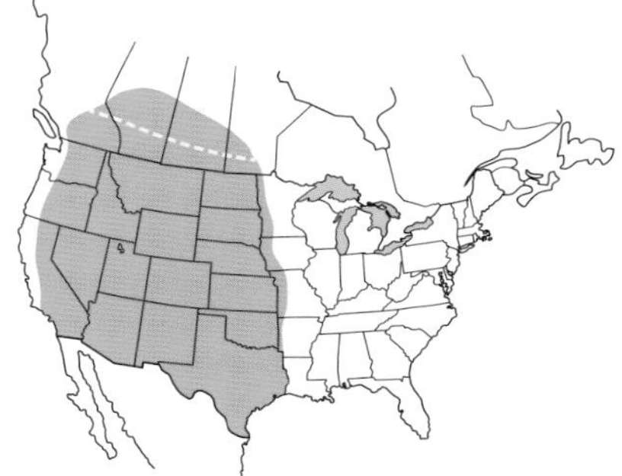

## ADDITIONAL HOST PLANT FOR:

Common checkered-skipper (*Pyrgus communis*), common streaky-skipper (*Celotes nessus*), laviana white-skipper (*Heliopetes laviana*), small checkered-skipper (*Pyrgus scriptura*), white checkered-skipper (*Pyrgus albescens*), Northern white-skipper (*Heliopetes ericetorum*), West Coast lady (*Vanessa annabella*)

| FLOWER COLOR | HEIGHT | AVAILABILITY |
|---|---|---|
| Red, orange | 1 to 4 feet (0.9 to 1.2 m) | Limited |

51.

ASTERACEAE

# Goldeneye

## *Bahiopsis* spp., Viguiera spp.

Showy sprays of yellow flowers, similar to small sunflowers, adorn this member of the sunflower family. With a native distribution in the Southwest and southern California, goldeneye is suitable for dry conditions and has an extended bloom period from late winter into fall, depending on the species. Because it offers early- and/or late-season nectar for monarchs, this is a great plant to include with other nectar plants in a monarch garden.

| EXPOSURE | SOIL MOISTURE | BLOOM TIME |
|---|---|---|
| Sun | Dry | Late winter, spring, summer, and fall |

## RECOMMENDED SPECIES

Monarchs have been observed nectaring on toothleaf goldeneye (*V. dentata*), Parish's goldeneye (*B. parishii*), and resinbush (*V. stenoloba*). Of these, resinbush is the most widely available commercially. Tornleaf goldeneye (*B. laciniata*) is a subshrub that can reach 10 feet (3 m) in height and provides evergreen foliage and a display of yellow flowers throughout most of the year for southern California locations.

## USES

**Ornamental**

**Neglected areas/tough sites**

**Hedgerow/screen/shade**

**Xeriscape**

## NATIVE RANGE

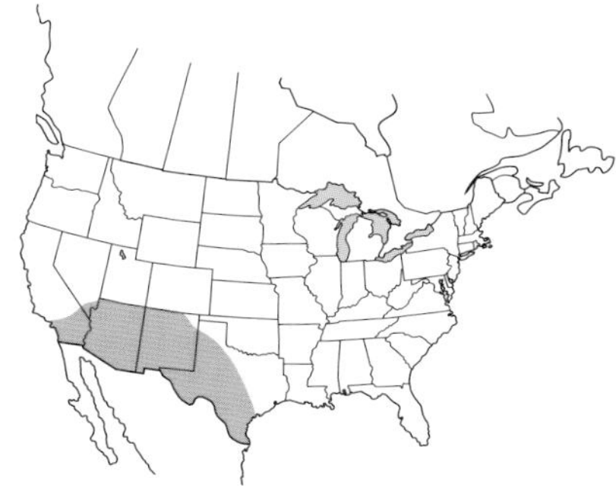

## ADDITIONAL HOST PLANT FOR:

Bordered patch butterfly (*Chlosyne lacinia*), California patch butterfly (*Chlosyne californica*), sunflower moth (*Homoeosoma electella*)

| FLOWER COLOR | HEIGHT | AVAILABILITY |
|---|---|---|
| Yellow | 3 to 10 feet (0.9 to 3 m) | Variable by region |

52.

ASTERACEAE

# Goldenrod, Goldentop

*Euthamia* spp., *Oligoneuron* spp., *Solidago* spp.

The name "goldenrod" is quite descriptive. Plants in this large group have stems that branch at the tops and hold hundreds to thousands of very small flower heads; each of those contains several tiny individual florets. They are all a rich yellow color and provide monarch butterflies with nectar in the late summer and fall, as the breeding season comes to a close and monarchs migrate to their overwintering grounds.

There are native goldenrod species in every part of North America, although fewer species in the West than in the East. In general, goldenrods

| EXPOSURE | SOIL MOISTURE | BLOOM TIME |
|---|---|---|
| Sun to part shade | Wet to average to dry | Late summer to fall |

thrive in open sunny spaces. Some are well adapted to disturbed soils or mowing, while others are quite sensitive and need stable, specific habitat conditions. There are also woodland goldenrods that do well in the shade.

## RECOMMENDED SPECIES

Some of the most recognizable species are showy goldenrod (*S. speciosa*), Riddell's goldenrod (*O. riddellii*), and stiff goldenrod (*O. rigidum*). Widely available from native plant nurseries, all are excellent butterfly and bee plants. Seaside goldenrod (*S. sempervirens*), a native of the Atlantic coast, blooms during the fall monarch butterfly migration and provides an important nectar source for the long journey. Grass-leaved goldenrod (*E. graminifolia*) grows well in lighter soils and supplies late-season nectar in flat-topped inflorescences.

## USES

**Ornamental**

**Wildflower meadow/prairie restoration**

**Neglected areas/tough sites**

**Rain garden/wetland/stormwater management**

**Xeriscape**

## NATIVE RANGE

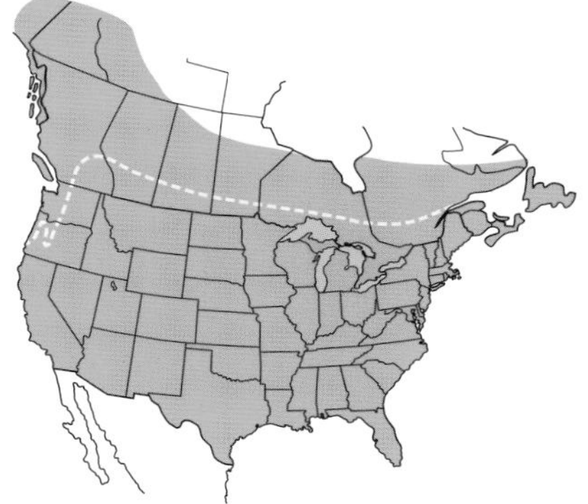

## ADDITIONAL HOST PLANT FOR:

Goldenrod gall moth (*Gnorimoschema gallaesolidaginis*), Northern checkerspot (*Chlosyne palla*), rockslide checkerspot (*Chlosyne whitneyi*)

| FLOWER COLOR | HEIGHT | AVAILABILITY |
| --- | --- | --- |
| Yellow | 1 to 6+ feet (0.9 to 1.8 m) | Wide |

53.

ASTERACEAE

# Gumweed

*Grindelia* spp.

Tough, resinous, and leathery-leaved, gumweeds are sometimes viewed as merely rangeland plants, but their glowing yellow blossoms are spectacularly showy, and they are among the best summer plants for monarchs and bees in the West. This is especially true along the West Coast, where many wildflowers bloom in spring immediately after the winter rains. Gumweed flowers, in contrast, provide critical nectar during summer and fall.

| EXPOSURE | SOIL MOISTURE | BLOOM TIME |
|---|---|---|
| Sun | Average to dry | Summer through late fall |

## RECOMMENDED SPECIES

In the dry inland West and across California, curlycup gumweed (*G. squarrosa*) is the most common and adaptable species. In the wet areas of the Pacific Northwest, Puget Sound gumweed (*G. integrifolia*) is better adapted and one of the best summer plants for attracting native bees in the region.

## USES

**Ornamental**

**Wildflower meadow/prairie restoration**

**Neglected areas/tough sites**

**Xeriscape**

## NATIVE RANGE

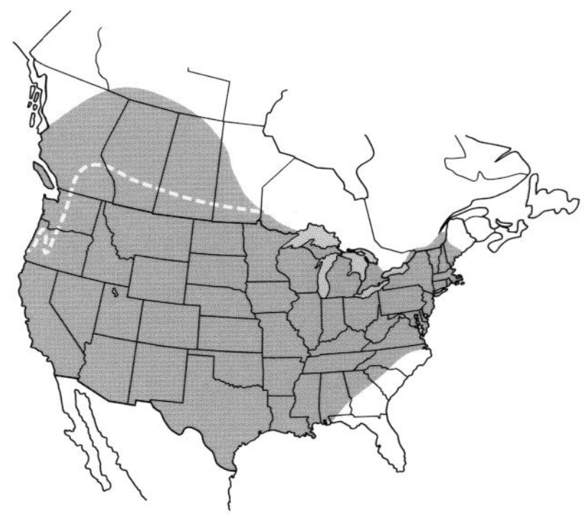

## ADDITIONAL HOST PLANT FOR:

Darker spotted straw moth (*Heliothis phloxiphaga*), tortrix moth (*Phaneta grindeliana*), and noctuid moth (*Schinia mortua*)

| FLOWER COLOR | HEIGHT | AVAILABILITY |
| --- | --- | --- |
| Yellow | 2 to 5 feet (0.6 to 1.5 m) | Wide |

54.

ASTERACEAE

# Ironweed

*Vernonia* spp.

Great and underrecognized companions for cup plant and wingstem, ironweeds grow similarly tall, and they favor the same rich, damp soils found on the edges of river-bottom forests, glades, and wet meadows.

Ironweeds tolerate occasional flooding and partial shade; their bitter foliage discourages deer and rabbit browsing. These traits, along with intensely magenta flowers, make them useful, beautiful species for stormwater management systems, shoreline revegetation, backyard water features, wetland reclamation, or simply for bold visual statements.

| EXPOSURE | SOIL MOISTURE | BLOOM TIME |
|---|---|---|
| Sun to part shade | Medium to wet | Summer to fall |

Under natural conditions, ironweeds benefit from occasional disturbance that creates new openings for the plants to spread, particularly because they often prefer the same soil conditions that support trees, which eventually shade them out. Ironweed plants may hybridize with each other, producing intermediate forms. As a side note, this genus also occurs in South America, Asia, and Africa, where a number of species develop into woody shrubs.

## RECOMMENDED SPECIES

The largest and showiest of ironweeds also tend to attract the most butterflies in gardens. Among these, New York ironweed (*V. noveboracensis*) is found across the eastern United States from New England to Florida and is very attractive to late-season monarchs. Giant ironweed (*V. gigantea*) has roughly the same range as New York ironweed, but it also occurs farther west into the Great Lakes region and the Mississippi River valley. Baldwin's ironweed (*V. baldwinii*), another very showy species, ranges farther south into the lower Mississippi River valley and southern Great Plains.

## USES

**Ornamental**

**Wildflower meadow/prairie restoration**

**Rain garden/wetland**

## ADDITIONAL HOST PLANT FOR:

American lady butterfly (*Vanessa virginiensis*)

## NATIVE RANGE

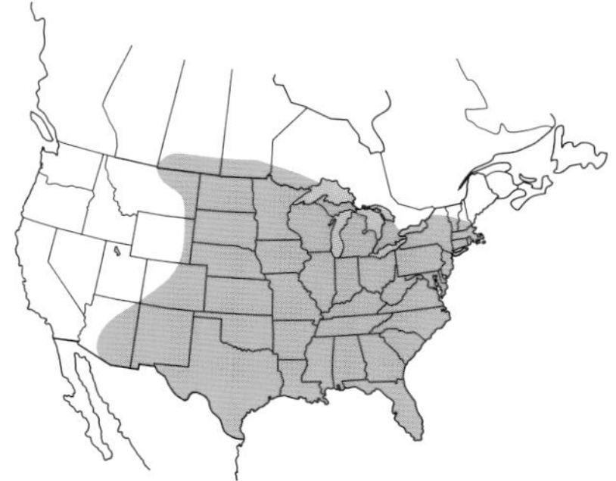

| FLOWER COLOR | HEIGHT | AVAILABILITY |
| --- | --- | --- |
| Purple | 2 to 8 feet (0.6 to 2.4 m) | Variable by region |

55.

CAMPANULACEAE

# Lobelia

*Lobelia* spp.

Native lobelias in North America produce intricate flowers arranged on spikes, and many species are very showy and colorful. The two commercially available species are among the larger members of the genus and produce the brightest blooms in partial shade. Both are adapted to moist soils, making them excellent for rain gardens and other wet sites. Hummingbirds pollinate cardinal flower; monarchs favor it for its nectar.

| EXPOSURE | SOIL MOISTURE | BLOOM TIME |
|---|---|---|
| Sun to part shade | Average to wet | Summer |

## RECOMMENDED SPECIES

There are more than two dozen native lobelias in North America, but only two are regularly available: great blue lobelia (*L. siphilitica*) and the red-blossomed cardinal flower (*L. cardinalis*).

## USES

**Ornamental**

**Wildflower meadow/prairie restoration**

**Rain garden/wetland/stormwater management**

## ADDITIONAL HOST PLANT FOR:

Dark-spotted palthis moth (*Palthis angulalis*)

## NATIVE RANGE

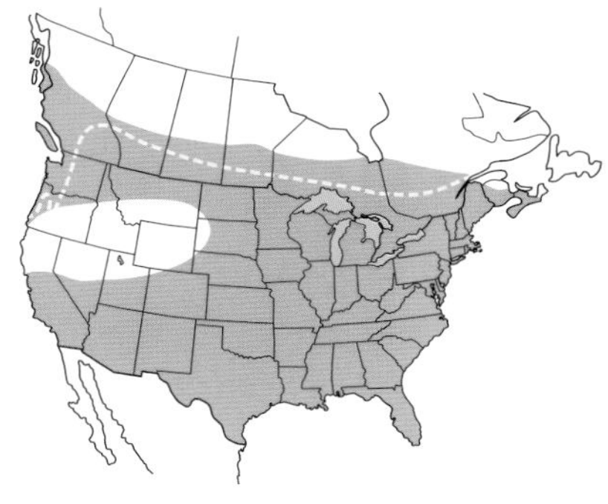

| FLOWER COLOR | HEIGHT | AVAILABILITY |
| --- | --- | --- |
| Red, blue | 2 to 4 feet (0.6 to 1.2 m) | Wide |

56.

ASTERACEAE

# Mistflower, Thoroughwort

*Conoclinium* spp.

In open and closed woodlands, mistflower is a perennial understory wildflower. The flower heads' fluffy disk florets are rich in nectar for late-summer and fall feeding. This plant is easy to establish and grow and can be used to fill in shady areas, but it also spreads relatively well on its own and may become too abundant.

| EXPOSURE | SOIL MOISTURE | BLOOM TIME |
|---|---|---|
| Sun to part shade | Moist to average | Late winter through fall (*C. greggii*); summer and fall (*C. coelestinum*) |

## RECOMMENDED SPECIES

Blue mistflower (*C. coelestinum*) is readily available through native plant nurseries in the south-central and southeastern United States and grows well in moist soils. Palmleaf thoroughwort (*C. greggii*) has a limited distribution in Texas and the Southwest; its leaves have an interesting palm-leaf shape.

## USES

**Ornamental**

**Hedgerow/screen/shade**

## ADDITIONAL HOST PLANT FOR:

*Nelphe carolina* moth, wavy-lined emerald moth (*Synchlora aerata*), Rawson's metalmark butterfly (*Calephelis rawsoni*)

## NATIVE RANGE

| FLOWER COLOR | HEIGHT | AVAILABILITY |
|---|---|---|
| Blue, white | 1 to 3 feet (0.3 to 0.9 m) | Wide |

57.

VERBENACEAE

# Mock Vervain

*Glandularia* spp.

The dense, highly ornamental flower clusters of mock vervain look almost too showy to be a wildflower. And because many of these species are uncommon (some found only in southern Texas), most gardeners don't know them.

Interestingly, several closely related nonnative members of the same genus (most from South America) are widely planted across the United States as garden ornamentals. Yet native mock vervains are just as showy, tolerant of dry conditions, and long blooming.

| EXPOSURE | SOIL MOISTURE | BLOOM TIME |
|---|---|---|
| Sun | Dry | Summer |

Members of this plant genus include both annual and perennial species, and several species are capable of hybridizing with each other. Compact and at home in garden beds, containers, and rock gardens, these plants are very compatible with landscapes that require a colorful and manicured appearance.

## RECOMMENDED SPECIES

There are 15 species of native mock vervain in the United States, mostly located in the desert Southwest and southern Great Plains. Some of the more common species with widespread occurrences include Dakota mock vervain (*G. bipinnatifida*), which is found from the Great Plains south to Central America and is an excellent grassland wildflower; rose mock vervain (*G. canadensis*), which is found in the lower Mississippi River valley; and Davis Mountain mock vervain (*G. wrightii*), a native of rocky canyons, sandy slopes, and grasslands from Texas to California.

## USES

**Ornamental**

**Containers**

**Wildflower meadow/prairie restoration**

**Neglected areas/tough sites**

**Xeriscape**

## NATIVE RANGE

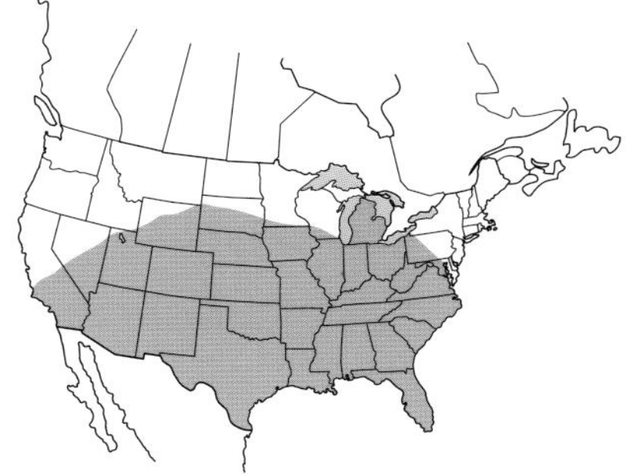

## ADDITIONAL HOST PLANT FOR:

No use as a host plant for other species is currently known.

| FLOWER COLOR | HEIGHT | AVAILABILITY |
| --- | --- | --- |
| Pink, purple | 1 to 2 feet (0.3 to 0.6 m) | Limited; variable by region |

58.

LAMIACEAE

# Mountainmint

*Pycnanthemum* spp.

Perennials that are native only to North America, these members of the mint family are close relatives of beebalm and have a strong, sweet, and very pleasant mint odor when the foliage is crushed. The flowers are small to tiny and arranged in clusters at the top of the plant; in some species the flowers grow along the stems next to the bases of leaves. Monarchs, other butterflies, and many native bees feed on the flowers' nectar.

| EXPOSURE | SOIL MOISTURE | BLOOM TIME |
|---|---|---|
| Sun to shade | Moist to average | Summer |

## RECOMMENDED SPECIES

Virginia mountainmint (*P. virginianum*) is the most widely available species, but roughly a dozen other locally adapted species can be found in eastern North America. For those in California, the native Sierra mint (*P. californicum*) is worth seeking out and does well in moist, shady sites and containers.

## USES

**Ornamental**

**Containers**

**Wildflower meadow/prairie restoration**

**Neglected areas/tough sites**

**Rain garden/wetland/stormwater management**

## ADDITIONAL HOST PLANT FOR:

Curved-toothed geometer moth (*Eutrapela clemataria*)

## NATIVE RANGE

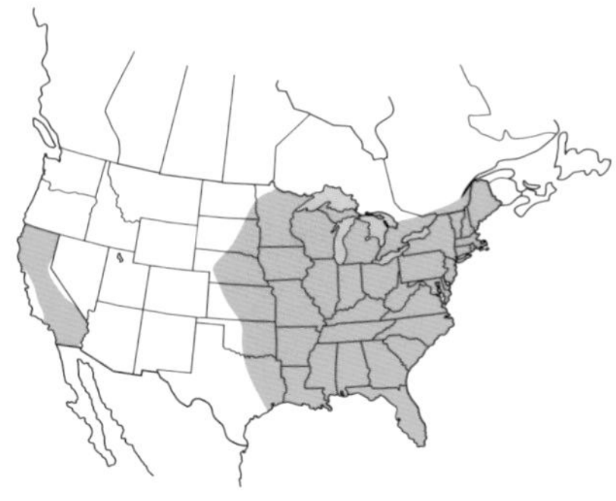

| FLOWER COLOR | HEIGHT | AVAILABILITY |
| --- | --- | --- |
| White | 4 feet (1.2 m) | Variable by region |

59.

ASTERACEAE

# Mule-ears

*Wyethia* spp.

These showy, slow-growing, long-lived plants belong to the same subtribe as the compass plant (*Silphium laciniatum*) and balsamroot (*Balsamorhiza* spp.), with similar thick, tough leaves and big sunflower-like blossoms. They are most at home on dry hillslopes and in open meadows.

In areas without plowing or heavy grazing, mule-ears can slowly spread to cover many acres, with deep taproots that allow them to survive periodic fires in their prime habitat. They are plants for expansive grassland landscapes, ideal where native bunch grasses are preferable to manicured lawns.

| EXPOSURE | SOIL MOISTURE | BLOOM TIME |
|---|---|---|
| Sun | Medium to dry | Spring |

Ten species of mule-ears are recognized, all occurring west of the Rocky Mountains. Of these, several are abundant only in the Great Basin, while a few are fairly common across multiple regions.

## RECOMMENDED SPECIES

The authors have had reasonably good success growing a few species of mule-ears from seed, although the plants seem to be finicky about transplanting. Some of the more adaptable species include narrowleaf mule-ears (*W. angustifolia*), which appears from Washington to California; woolly mule-ears (*W. mollis*), native to inland California and Nevada; and Northern mule-ears (*W. amplexicaulis*), ranging across much of the inland West from British Columbia south into the Great Basin.

## USES

**Ornamental**

**Wildflower meadow/prairie restoration**

**Neglected areas/tough sites**

**Xeriscape**

## NATIVE RANGE

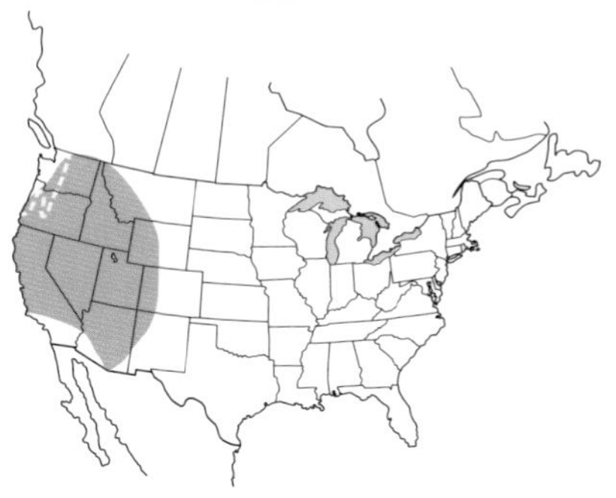

## ADDITIONAL HOST PLANT FOR:

Omnivorous leaftier moth (*Cnephasia longana*)

| FLOWER COLOR | HEIGHT | AVAILABILITY |
|---|---|---|
| Yellow, white | 1 to 3 feet (0.3 to 0.9 m) | Limited |

60.

ASTERACEAE

# Native Thistles

*Cirsium* spp.

Not to be confused with widespread invasive species such as Canada thistle (*C. arvense*), more than 60 native thistles, including many that are now rare or uncommon, grow in the United States and Canada. Unfortunately, long-term efforts to eradicate troublesome thistles have led to mistaken or accidental assaults on the beneficial, beautiful, and nonaggressive wild thistles that used to grace natural areas. Only recently have ecologists and native plant gardeners begun to pay more attention to these interesting

| EXPOSURE | SOIL MOISTURE | BLOOM TIME |
|---|---|---|
| Sun to part shade | Medium to dry | Summer |

plants, which support a huge range of pollinators as well as seed-feeding songbirds such as indigo buntings.

In monitoring insect visitation to different types of wildflowers, ecologists have recorded some of the greatest insect abundance and diversity on thistles. These species range from tough desert-adapted varieties to specimens found only in wetlands or Great Lakes sand dunes, as well as woodland-edge plants that require deep, fertile soils.

There is an interesting native thistle for almost every planting situation, although finding them from nurseries can be a challenge. Because of their very high monarch attractiveness, this group represents a "must-have" for any serious butterfly garden.

## USES

**Ornamental**

**Wildflower meadow/prairie restoration**

**Xeriscape**

## NATIVE RANGE

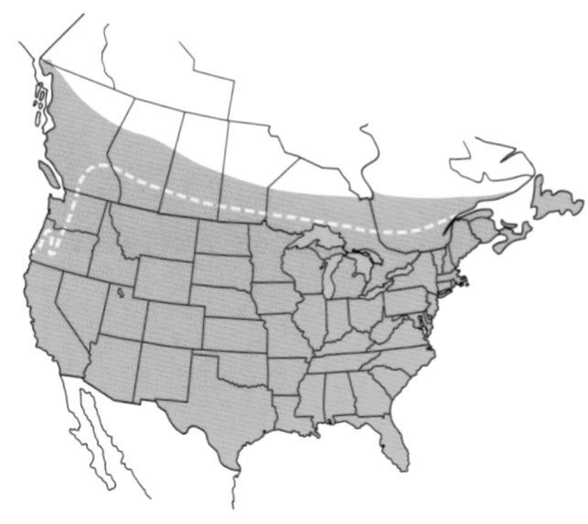

## ADDITIONAL HOST PLANT FOR:

The little metalmark (*Calephelis virginiensis*) is a southeastern butterfly that uses yellow thistle (*C. horridulum*) as its host plant. The midwestern butterfly swamp metalmark (*Calephelis muticum*) uses swamp thistle (*C. muticum*) and tall thistle (*C. altissimum*). In the West, the pale crescent (*Phyciodes pallida*) and Mylitta crescent (*Phyciodes mylitta*) caterpillars feed on thistles, as does the rare California crescent (*Phyciodes orseis*).

| FLOWER COLOR | HEIGHT | AVAILABILITY |
| --- | --- | --- |
| Pink, purple, white | 8 feet (2.4 m) | Limited; variable by region |

## RECOMMENDED SPECIES

Cobweb thistle (*C. occidentale*), a pretty, magenta-flowered plant found primarily in California, is unique for its foliage, which is covered in fine, soft hairs. Field thistle (*C. discolor*), common across the Midwest and Northeast, has interesting leaves with almost white undersides and is a magnet for monarchs, large bumblebees, and a huge range of prairie butterflies. Tall thistle (*C. altissimum*), which, as the name implies, can reach up to 8 feet (2.4 m) in height, ranges from the Appalachian Mountains to the Great Plains and is documented as the single most visited late-season monarch nectar plant in some locations.

61.

LAMIACEAE

# Obedient Plant, False Dragonhead

*Physostegia* spp.

Also known as lionsheart or false dragonhead, obedient plant is a brilliantly showy member of the mint family that can spread aggressively when located in optimal conditions. It prefers full sun combined with cool, damp, richly organic soils, such as poorly drained meadow depressions or the edges of prairie ponds. Obedient plant struggles in dry or hot locations, where its

| EXPOSURE | SOIL MOISTURE | BLOOM TIME |
| --- | --- | --- |
| Sun | Medium to wet | Summer |

lower leaves tend to turn yellow and curl and its normally robust rhizomatous root system spreads only minimally.

Although not as adaptable as some species, this can be an outstanding ornamental plant under the right conditions, and is a great option for rain gardens, bioswales, and damp, unmown ditches. Obedient plant has an expansive native range, occurring throughout southeastern Canada, the eastern United States as far south as Florida, and Texas. Its name refers to individual flowers' tendency to remain in place when they are pushed to one side.

## RECOMMENDED SPECIES

Several cultivated varieties of obedient plant have been developed, many of which have darker pink or lavender flowers than the wild-type species. In addition, several other members of this genus occur throughout temperate North America, although none appears to be commercially available.

## USES

**Ornamental**

**Wildflower meadow/prairie restoration**

**Rain garden/wetland**

## ADDITIONAL HOST PLANT FOR:

Verbena bud moth (*Endothenia hebesana*)

## NATIVE RANGE

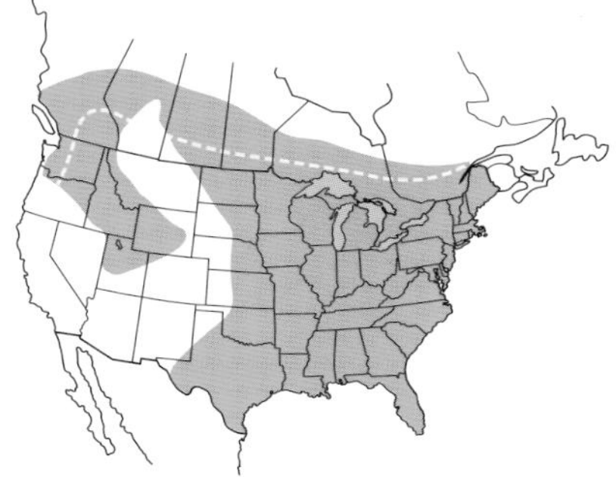

| FLOWER COLOR | HEIGHT | AVAILABILITY |
|---|---|---|
| White, pink | 1 to 4 feet (0.3 to 1.2 m) | Variable by region |

62.

## SCROPHULARIACEAE/ PLANTAGINACEAE

# Penstemon

*Penstemon* spp.

Known by the common names beardtongue and penstemon, this genus is the most diverse group of native North American wildflowers. They occur across a wide variety of habitats, and nearly all are excellent pollinator plants, with attractive flowers. The types of pollinators they attract vary depending on the species; some showy red-flowered penstemons attract hummingbirds, and others support sphinx moths. The largest are tall enough to plant on the edges of hedgerows in the West. Smaller species

| EXPOSURE | SOIL MOISTURE | BLOOM TIME |
|---|---|---|
| Sun to part shade | Moist to average to dry | Summer |

work well as meadow plants, especially among smaller grasses that will not shade them out. The average sugar concentration in the nectar of some penstemon species has been reported at 37 percent.

## RECOMMENDED SPECIES

In the West, Venus penstemon (*P. venustus*), showy penstemon (*P. spectabilis*), Palmer's penstemon (*P. palmeri*), firecracker penstemon (*P. eatonii*). In the East, foxglove beardtongue (*P. digitalis*) and large beardtongue (*P. grandiflorus*).

---

## USES

**Ornamental**

**Containers**

**Wildflower meadow/prairie restoration**

**Neglected areas/tough sites**

**Hedgerow/screen/shade**

**Xeriscape**

## NATIVE RANGE

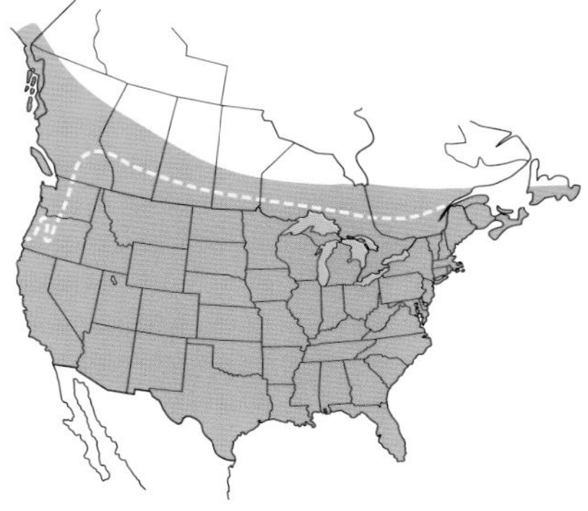

## ADDITIONAL HOST PLANT FOR:

Chalcedon checkerspot (*Euphydryas chalcedona*), Baltimore checkerspot (*Euphydryas phaeton*—uncommon), arachne checkerspot (*Poladryas arachne*), dotted checkerspot (*Poladryas minuta*), and Edith's checkerspot (*Euphydryas editha*) butterflies

| FLOWER COLOR | HEIGHT | AVAILABILITY |
|---|---|---|
| White, pink, purple, red | 1 to 4 feet (0.3 to 1.2 m) | Wide |

63.

POLEMONIACEAE

# Phlox

*Phlox* spp.

More than 60 species of phlox occur in North America, with several found in nearly every ecosystem from boreal forests and alpine meadows to southwestern deserts and southeastern pine forests. Most of these habitat specialists tend to be locally uncommon, however, and sometimes rare, occurring primarily in areas with minimal human disturbance.

A few species, such as common garden phlox (*P. paniculata*) and carpet phlox (*P. canescens*), have been developed into ornamental cultivars and now appear in gardens from coast to coast. Most have large, showy flower

| EXPOSURE | SOIL MOISTURE | BLOOM TIME |
|---|---|---|
| Sun to shade | Medium to dry | Summer |

clusters, while the plants are either tall, upright, and multistemmed or low growing and creeping, forming ground-covering mats.

Some gardeners feel these diverse, mostly perennial plants are slow to establish and finicky about their placement; they can also be popular with deer and rabbits. Yet once established, phlox tend to live long lives and spread slowly into multistemmed clumps. These fine plants attract big swallowtail butterflies and hummingbird-like hawk moths, and passing monarchs will certainly nectar from them as well.

## RECOMMENDED SPECIES

The number and diversity of phlox species is staggering, with many hybrids and cultivated varieties available. We have not seen any evidence that the "improved" ornamentals are better for butterflies than wild varieties, and they may be worse. Look for true wild-type plants such as wild blue phlox (*P. divaricata*) and prairie phlox (*P. pilosa*), both of which occur across most of the eastern United States and southeastern Canada. In the arid West, longleaf phlox (*P. longifolia*) and mountain phlox (*P. austromontana*) are lower-growing species of rocky canyons and scrubby desert foothills. Both are hard to find but well suited for rock gardens and xeriscaping.

## USES

**Ornamental**

**Wildflower meadow/prairie restoration**

**Xeriscape**

## ADDITIONAL HOST PLANT FOR:

Phlox moth (*Schinia indiana*) and common idia moth (*Idia aemula*)

## NATIVE RANGE

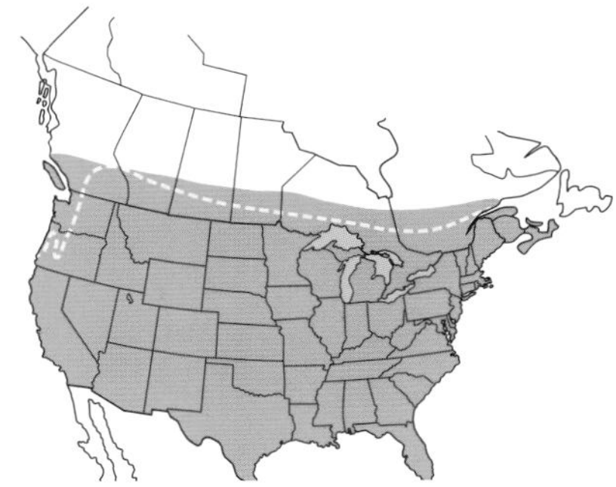

| FLOWER COLOR | HEIGHT | AVAILABILITY |
| --- | --- | --- |
| Pink, white, lavender, blue | 6 to 24 inches (15 to 61 cm) | Variable by region |

64.

ASTERACEAE

# Purple Coneflower

*Echinacea* spp.

With colorful daisylike flowers, purple coneflowers make beautiful additions to ornamental gardens as well as wildflower meadows and butterfly gardens. Purple coneflowers have an extended bloom period, are tolerant of a range of conditions, and display spiky seed heads that remain into the winter, when they provide visual interest and a food source for seed-eating birds. All purple coneflowers attract a variety of bees and butterflies. In addition to monarchs, many other butterflies sip nectar from the flowers, including swallowtails and sulphurs.

| EXPOSURE | SOIL MOISTURE | BLOOM TIME |
|---|---|---|
| Sun | Average to dry | Summer |

## RECOMMENDED SPECIES

Common purple coneflower (*E. purpurea*) tends to be the most adaptable and commercially available of the various coneflowers. Pale purple coneflower (*E. pallida*) and narrow-leaved coneflower (*E. angustifolia*) also attract many pollinators. All are relatively slow growing and take several years to begin flowering when grown from seed, but they can be extremely long-lived plants under optimal conditions.

## USES

**Ornamental**

**Containers**

**Wildflower meadow/prairie restoration**

**Neglected areas/tough sites**

## NATIVE RANGE

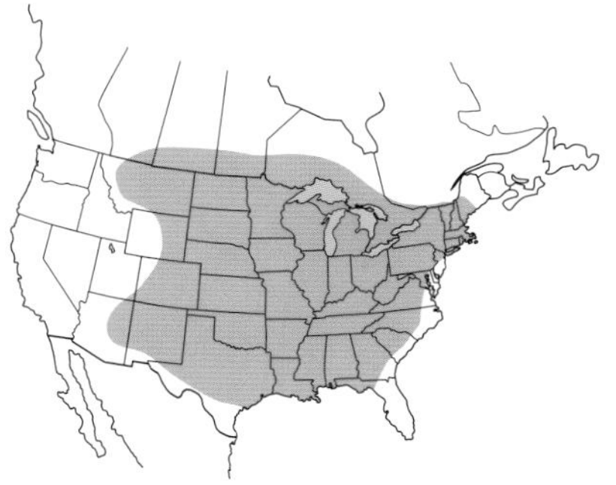

## ADDITIONAL HOST PLANT FOR:

Sunflower moth (*Homoeosoma electella*)

| FLOWER COLOR | HEIGHT | AVAILABILITY |
|---|---|---|
| Purple | 2 to 4 feet (0.6 to 1.2 m) | Wide |

65.

ASTERACEAE

# Ragwort, Groundsel

*Packera* spp., *Senecio* spp.

The common name "ragwort" might not sound very elegant, but species in this genus are cheerful and visually appealing. The flowers are daisy-like, with yellow rays around a center of yellow florets. The diversity of leaf arrangement, shape, and color gives this group a lot of garden design potential. And monarchs nectar on them!

| EXPOSURE | SOIL MOISTURE | BLOOM TIME |
|---|---|---|
| Sun | Average | Spring to summer |

## RECOMMENDED SPECIES

Several species of this perennial wildflower can be planted for monarch and pollinator habitat: threadleaf ragwort (*S. flaccidus*), lambstongue ragwort (*S. integerrimus*), broom-like ragwort (*S. spartioides*), arrowleaf ragwort (*S. triangularis*), and golden ragwort (*P. aurea*).

## USES

**Ornamental**

**Wildflower meadow/prairie restoration**

**Neglected areas/tough sites**

**Xeriscape**

## NATIVE RANGE

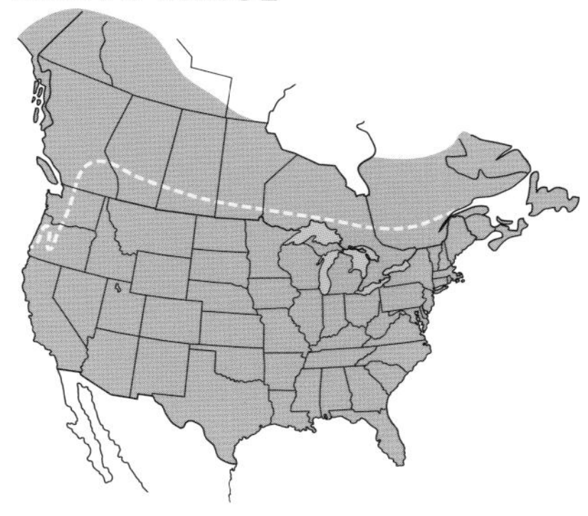

## ADDITIONAL HOST PLANT FOR:

Northern metalmark (*Calephelis borealis*)

| FLOWER COLOR | HEIGHT | AVAILABILITY |
|---|---|---|
| Yellow or orange | 1 to 2 feet (0.3 to 0.6 m) | Variable by region |

66.

APIACEAE

# Rattlesnake Master, Eryngo

*Eryngium* spp.

Globelike, spiky blossoms and silvery, tough, sometimes spiny leaves give these members of the carrot family a striking appearance that can be used to great design effect in gardens and meadow plantings. The genus includes both perennial and annual species that are adaptable to a variety of habitats.

Perennial rattlesnake master (*E. yuccifolium*) is a prairie native commonly available from native plant nurseries. Its scientific name refers to the

| EXPOSURE | SOIL MOISTURE | BLOOM TIME |
|---|---|---|
| Sun to part shade | Moist to dry | Summer |

plant's yuccalike leaves, while the common name supposedly refers to its historic use as a home remedy for rattlesnake bites (not recommended!). Another theory about the common name is that the plant was part of a ceremony to honor or seek protection from rattlesnakes. Rattlesnake master's thick, hollow stems are slow to break down and provide nest sites for tunnel-nesting bees.

## RECOMMENDED SPECIES

In the southern Plains, Leavenworth's eryngo (*E. leavenworthii*) is a beautiful annual with lavender flowers that rival any cultivated ornamental. Across much of the United States, the introduced sea holly (*E. maritimum*) is a common flower garden plant with blue foliage and blossoms; like its native relatives, it attracts many bees. In addition to providing nectar and a good perch for monarch butterflies, rattlesnake master attracts many small sweat bees, syrphid flies, beneficial wasps, and black-and-gold bumblebees (*Bombus auricomus*). It is also a caterpillar host plant for the endangered rattlesnake master borer moth (*Coleotechnites eryngiella*).

## USES

**Ornamental**

**Wildflower meadow/prairie restoration**

## ADDITIONAL HOST PLANT FOR:

The rattlesnake master borer moth (*Papaipema eryngii*) is a rare prairie moth that has been considered for protection under the federal Endangered Species Act. It is dependent on rattlesnake master as its host plant.

## NATIVE RANGE

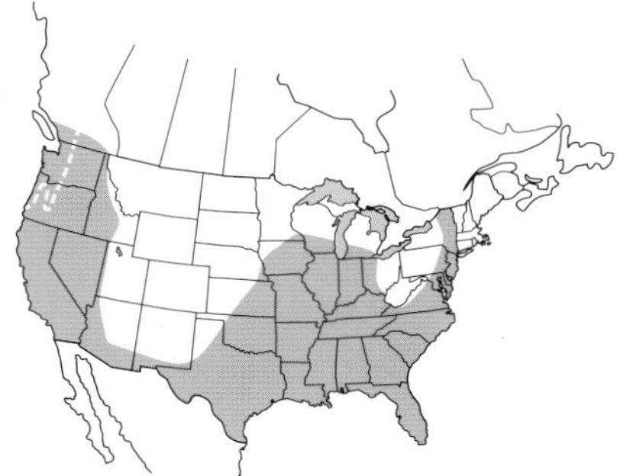

| FLOWER COLOR | HEIGHT | AVAILABILITY |
|---|---|---|
| White, blue, purple | 6 feet (1.8 m) | Wide |

# 67.

## ASTERACEAE

# Rosinweed, Prairie Dock, Compass Plant, Cup Plant

*Silphium* spp.

These huge, sunflower-like prairie plants have deep taproots and enormous, rough, and papery leaves, and are some of the longest-living wildflowers in the regions where they occur. Although they have widely disappeared from natural areas (a story chronicled by Aldo Leopold in his essay "A Prairie Birthday"), they are beloved by prairie restorationists and native plant gardeners in the Midwest and are now commonly used in native plant landscaping.

The tall stature of these plants makes them most valuable as background for smaller species, as tall screens (to hide your compost bin!), or in expansive prairies where the flower heads form convenient perches for songbirds (which also enjoy the seeds throughout the winter). All of these plants produce multiple flowers on each stem, which attract a continuous parade of fascinating insects. Beyond monarchs, these are great plants for watching other butterflies, including various prairie skippers, as well as many types of wild bees, soldier beetles, and more.

| EXPOSURE | SOIL MOISTURE | BLOOM TIME |
|---|---|---|
| Sun | Medium to dry | Summer |

| FLOWER COLOR | HEIGHT | AVAILABILITY |
|---|---|---|
| Yellow | 4 to 7 feet (1.2 to 2.1 m) | Variable by region |

## RECOMMENDED SPECIES

Cup plant (*S. perfoliatum*) is the most widely distributed and well-known member of this genus, favoring moist, fertile soils across the central United States, the Northeast, and southern Ontario. It tends to form large colonies (slowly) when it finds a location where it can thrive. The stem-clasping leaves hold rainwater, making the plant a natural birdbath and vertical frog pond. Compass plant (*S. laciniatum*) has deeply lobed leaves that typically align on a north–south axis, giving the plant its common name. Starry rosinweed (*S. asteriscus*) occurs throughout the Deep South, including southern Florida, and is a reliable magnet for big, showy butterflies, monarchs, queens, swallowtails, and more.

A number of other species in this genus exist, including a few with small native ranges. All are structurally and visually fascinating and wonderful butterfly plants, many with large and striking foliage.

## USES

**Ornamental**

**Wildflower meadow/prairie restoration**

**Hedgerow/screen/shade**

## ADDITIONAL HOST PLANT FOR:

Rosinweed moth (*Tebenna silphiella*) larvae feed on the leaves of *S. integrifolium*. (Considering the sandpaperlike texture of these leaves, that's impressive.)

## NATIVE RANGE

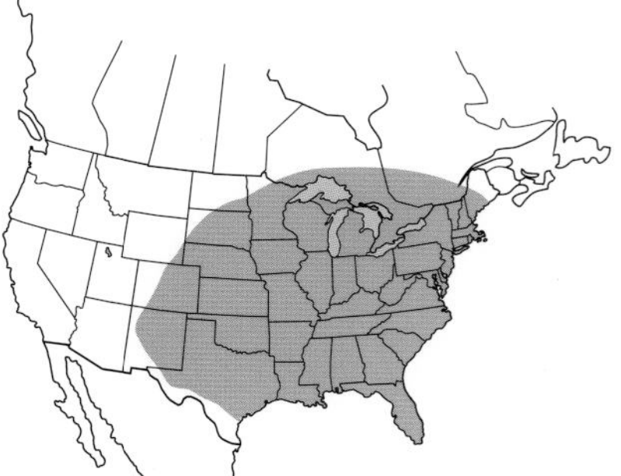

68.

LAMIACEAE

# Salvia

*Salvia* spp.

A very diverse group of annual and perennial, herbaceous and shrubby species, this genus also includes several nonnatives. To make matters more confusing, they are sometimes referred to as sage, although they are unrelated to sagebrush (*Artemisia* spp.).

The true native salvias are considered excellent bee, butterfly, and hummingbird plants: Many have very long bloom times and can produce copious amounts of nectar. Although there are around 50 salvia in the United States (and one in the arid region of inland British Columbia), they are most

| EXPOSURE | SOIL MOISTURE | BLOOM TIME |
|---|---|---|
| Sun | Medium to dry | Summer |

common in the desert Southwest and parts of Texas. The more temperate and cold-climate species tend to be smaller, less diverse, and far less common. The value of this diverse group of plants is probably greatest in warm, dry, or Mediterranean climates where they are nearly always drought-hardy and excellent for low-water landscaping.

## RECOMMENDED SPECIES

Western monarchs in California benefit from robust, shrubby species such as black sage (*S. mellifera*), a fantastic nectar producer that attracts a dizzying array of flower visitors. Farther into the arid inland West, desert chia (*S. columbariae*) is a reliable desert-adapted wildflower. Outside the West, perennial blue sage (*S. azurea*) is a beautiful wildflower of roadsides and pastures found in the southern Great Plains, Ozarks, Gulf Coast, and into Florida. It is probably underutilized as a garden plant, given its attractive clear blue flowers and tenacity in dry soils. It's also hardier in colder climates than those where it occurs naturally.

## USES

**Ornamental**

**Containers**

**Wildflower meadow/prairie restoration**

**Xeriscape**

## NATIVE RANGE

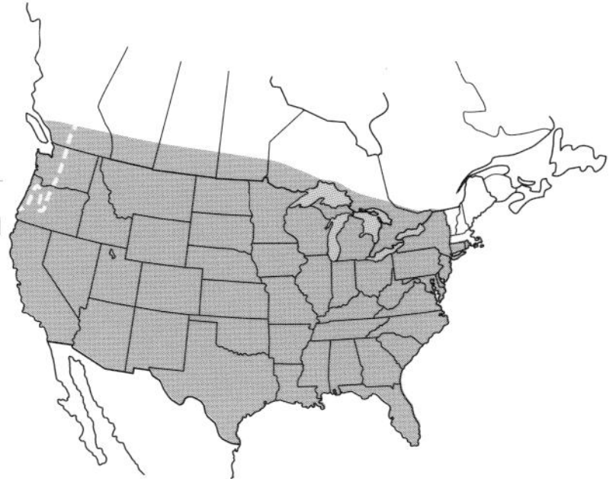

## ADDITIONAL HOST PLANT FOR:

Hermit sphinx moth (*Lintneria eremitus*). In California and south into Mexico, other uncommon moths in the genera *Anstenoptilia, Sphinx,* and *Pherne* feed on salvia species as host plants.

| FLOWER COLOR | HEIGHT | AVAILABILITY |
| --- | --- | --- |
| Blue, purple, pink, white, red | 1 to 4 feet (0.3 to 1.2 m) | Variable by region |

69.

NYCTAGINACEAE

# Sand Verbena

*Abronia* spp.

Although also called wild lantana, plants in this group are neither verbena nor lantana; rather, they are members of the four o'clock family (Nyctaginaceae). These western plants of sandy, dry areas tend to be rare.

The leaves are broad, smooth, and leathery, adapted to the arid and tough conditions of coast and desert. The flowers are long-lived and borne in rounded clusters that provide a display of color and source of nectar.

| EXPOSURE | SOIL MOISTURE | BLOOM TIME |
|---|---|---|
| Sun | Dry | Some species year-round; others in a distinct season |

## RECOMMENDED SPECIES

Coastal sand verbena (*A. latifolia*) is a low-growing perennial with yellow flowers that grows along the Pacific coast and can provide nectar to monarch adults as they come out of overwintering. Pink sand verbena (*A. umbellata*) is a showy plant with range and habitat requirements similar to coastal sand verbena. For the Southwest, desert sand verbena (*A. villosa*) is an annual species, also quite showy, with some limited commercial availability.

## USES

**Ornamental**

**Neglected areas/tough sites**

**Xeriscape**

## ADDITIONAL HOST PLANT FOR:

Some moths in the genera *Psammopolia* and *Lithariapteryx*. *Abronia* is primarily a nectar plant, however.

## NATIVE RANGE

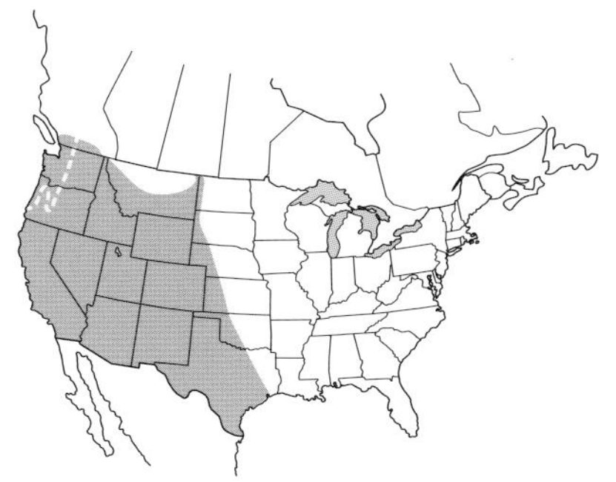

| FLOWER COLOR | HEIGHT | AVAILABILITY |
|---|---|---|
| Yellow, pink, purple | 6 to 72 inches (15 to 183 cm) | Variable by region |

70.

ASTERACEAE

# Smooth Oxeye, False Sunflower

*Heliopsis* spp.

This yellow-flowered, daisylike plant is native in meadows and prairies ranging from the southern Maritime Provinces of eastern Canada south to the Gulf Coast, and across the Midwest. It's potentially one of the most carefree wildflowers in eastern North America and is happy in most sunny locations with adequate soil moisture and fertile organic matter.

| EXPOSURE | SOIL MOISTURE | BLOOM TIME |
|---|---|---|
| Full sun | Medium | Summer |

Although the plants are mostly clump-forming, the clumps do expand over time, and an abundance of foliage fills out the stem clusters, making it very effective at crowding out other weedy plants in low-maintenance mass plantings. While this is probably not one of the most attractive plants to butterflies that we've observed, monarchs do visit it for nectar when it is in bloom, and its reliability and ease of establishment make it a great plant to include in prairie gardens.

## RECOMMENDED SPECIES

Some false sunflower cultivars are available, although they are probably all inferior as butterfly plants compared to the wild type. Two other native species in the genus also exist in the United States, with limited ranges. These include smooth oxeye (*H. gracilis*), which is uncommon from Texas to South Carolina. The even less common mountain oxeye (*H. parvifolia*) is limited to extreme southern Texas, New Mexico, and Arizona.

## USES

**Ornamental**

**Wildflower meadow/prairie restoration**

## ADDITIONAL HOST PLANT FOR:

Sunflower moth (*Homoeosoma electella*), *Carmenta ithacae* moth

## NATIVE RANGE

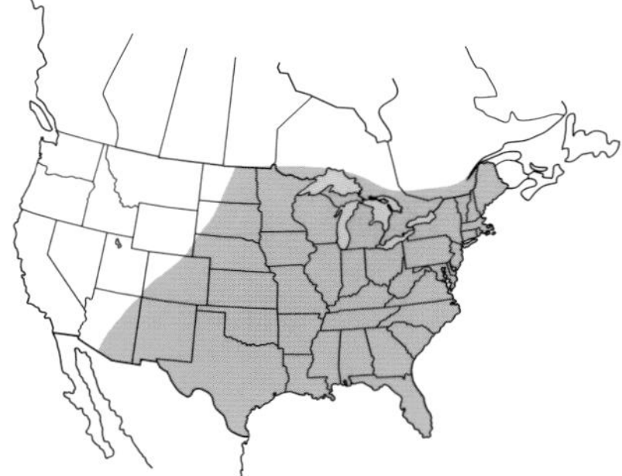

| FLOWER COLOR | HEIGHT | AVAILABILITY |
|---|---|---|
| Yellow | 3 to 5 feet (0.9 to 1.5 m) | Variable by region; wide |

71.

ASTERACEAE

# Snakeroot

*Ageratina* spp.

Ranging from New England to the Midwest and south to the Gulf Coast, white snakeroot (*A. altissima*) is one of the most common and widely spread native wildflowers, especially along woodland edges, shady vacant lots, damp river bottoms, and similar overgrown locations. It is so common, in fact, that it's sometimes regarded as weedy, a reputation bolstered by the leaves' superficial resemblance to stinging nettle, the modest white flowers, and the plant's network of rhizomes that send up new shoots, creating small colonies in optimal locations.

| EXPOSURE | SOIL MOISTURE | BLOOM TIME |
|---|---|---|
| Partial shade to shade | Damp to dry | Summer |

Yet this humble plant, so tolerant of neglect, shade, compacted soil, and other tough conditions, is a reliable nectar source. It attracts monarchs and other flower visitors, such as leafcutter bees and a surprising number of moth species, including several moths that feed on white snakeroot foliage. A relative of boneset and joe pye weed, snakeroot is a good choice for shaded locations where those related species may be more difficult to grow.

Because of its widespread distribution, and because it's not the most glamorous species, white snakeroot may have limited commercial availability. However, for the average gardener who finds this species already growing in an overgrown corner of the yard, it's one to foster and observe closely for the interesting insect activity it supports.

## RECOMMENDED SPECIES

No known varieties or ornamental selections exist for white snakeroot, although several other members of the *Ageratina* genus are found across North America, including fragrant snakeroot (*A. aromatica*) in the Southeast and western snakeroot (*A. occidentalis*) in the Great Basin and West Coast. Although less is known about the pollinator relationships of these species, they all may be excellent monarch nectar plants.

## USES

**Neglected areas/tough sites**

**Hedgerow/screen/shade**

**Rain garden/wetland/stormwater management**

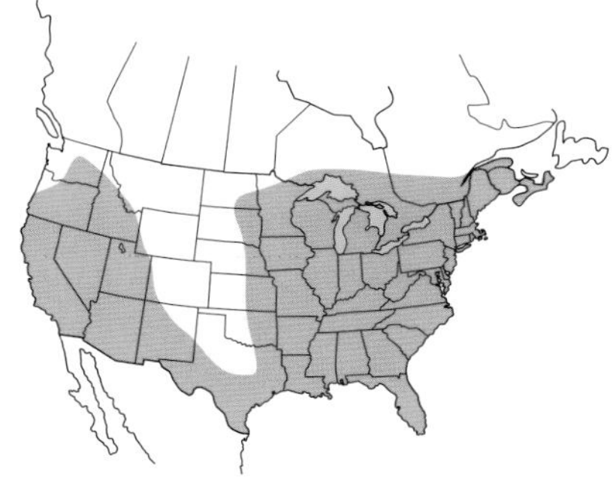

## ADDITIONAL HOST PLANT FOR:

*Leucospilaptery × venustella*, a moth with strikingly "feathered" scales on the wings

| FLOWER COLOR | HEIGHT | AVAILABILITY |
| --- | --- | --- |
| White | 3 feet (0.9 m) | Variable by region |

72.

ASTERACEAE

# Sneezeweed

*Helenium* spp.

In natural settings, sneezeweed is a plant of silty, wet soils, such as river-bottom meadows, sunny floodplains, and the edges of seasonal ponds. Its long-lasting flowers bloom late in the season, providing a reliable nectar source when most other wildflowers have finished blooming and are beginning to go dormant. This late bloom can be a valuable resource for fall-migrating monarchs, as well as bumblebee queens preparing for winter dormancy.

| EXPOSURE | SOIL MOISTURE | BLOOM TIME |
| --- | --- | --- |
| Sun | Wet | Fall |

Aside from being well suited to wetland gardens and damp locations, these plants are also excellent for settings with heavy deer, rabbit, or livestock browsing—the foliage is harshly bitter and grazing animals avoid it.

Despite the name, sneezeweed does not actually cause sneezing. Beekeepers know it to be a prolific honey plant, but its bitter, unpalatable honey is useful only for feeding overwintering bees.

## RECOMMENDED SPECIES

Twenty species of sneezeweed occur across the United States and southern Canada, but most are uncommon and not commercially available. Common sneezeweed (*H. autumnale*) is found across most of the United States and southern Canada and is sometimes commercially available as seed or transplants. The showy purplehead sneezeweed (*H. flexuosum*) occurs only in the eastern United States and is less common but visually appealing.

## USES

**Ornamental**

**Wildflower meadow/prairie restoration**

**Rain garden/wetland**

## ADDITIONAL HOST PLANT FOR:

Aster borer moth (*Papaipema impecuniosa*), *Carmenta ithacae*

## NATIVE RANGE

| FLOWER COLOR | HEIGHT | AVAILABILITY |
| --- | --- | --- |
| Yellow | 1 to 5 feet (0.3 to 1.5 m) | Variable by region; wide |

# 73.

## ASTERACEAE

# Sunflower

## *Helianthus* spp.

Hooray for *Helianthus*, literally "sunflower" from the Greek. Perhaps no other flower represents summer in North America as well as the cheerful, adaptable, and multiform sunflowers, one of our most diverse and widespread natives. Many sunflower species and horticultural varieties are available, and all support a tremendous diversity of insects, including of course monarchs, other butterflies, bees, wasps, flies, and pollen-feeding soldier beetles. The average sugar concentration in the nectar of sunflower species reportedly ranges from 31 to 49 percent.

Look more closely at a sunflower's flower and you'll see that it is made up of a few to hundreds of individual florets. Each little floret tube has a male phase (when pollen is available) and a female phase (when the antennae-like stigmas are receptive to pollen). When a pollinator—a monarch, bee, or fly—moves the pollen from flower to flower, pollination occurs and the familiar sunflower seed will develop, one seed per floret.

### RECOMMENDED SPECIES

The dozens of native perennial sunflowers have smaller flower heads but share the design and biology of the annual common sunflower (*H. annuus*). Avoid pollenless or double-petaled ornamental varieties, as they don't offer the food monarchs or pollinators need.

Prairie sunflower (*H. petiolaris*) is an annual that is multibranched and not as tall as the common annual sunflower. Tall Maximilian sunflower (*H. maximiliani*) is suited to dry sunny sites, especially in the Great Plains,

| EXPOSURE | SOIL MOISTURE | BLOOM TIME |
|---|---|---|
| Shade to sun | Moist to average to dry | Late summer to autumn |

| FLOWER COLOR | HEIGHT | AVAILABILITY |
|---|---|---|
| Yellow, orange | 8 feet (2.4 m) | Wide |

where it can be very long-lived once established. Woodland sunflower (*H. divaricatus*) is a perennial suited to shady locations in the eastern United States and Canada. Downy sunflower (*H. mollis*) forms 3- to 4-foot-high (0.9 to 1.2 m) masses of gray-green, wide, opposite leaves topped by yellow flowers. For moist sites, sawtooth sunflower (*H. grosseserratus*) will fill the space with hundreds of tall (over 6 feet, or 1.8 m) bright flowers swaying in the breeze. Other species occur in the Great Basin and California; all are excellent pollinator plants.

## USES

**Ornamental**

**Wildflower meadow/prairie restoration**

**Neglected areas/tough sites**

**Hedgerow/screen/shade**

**Rain garden/wetland/stormwater management**

**Xeriscape**

## NATIVE RANGE

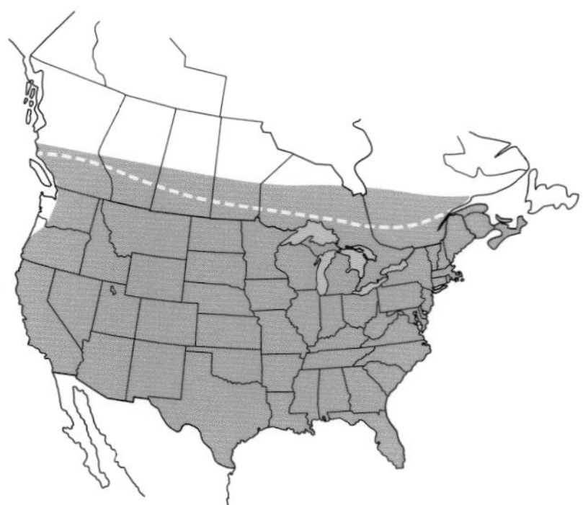

## ADDITIONAL HOST PLANT FOR:

Gorgone checkerspot (*Chlosyne gorgone*), silvery checkerspot (*Chlosyne nycteis*), and bordered patch (*Chlosyne lacinia*) butterflies

# 74.

## ASTERACEAE

# Sweetscent, Camphorweed

*Pluchea* spp.

As the common names imply, plants in the genus *Pluchea* smell good. The disk flowers provide nectar; glands on the plant give it its medicinal scent. The genus is large, but for North America the most common species are the showy annuals of coastal marshlands that tolerate light salinity and require moist soil. They are excellent plants for pollinators and other beneficial insects.

| EXPOSURE | SOIL MOISTURE | BLOOM TIME |
|---|---|---|
| Sun to shade | Moist | Summer to fall |

## RECOMMENDED SPECIES

Sweetscent (*P. odorata*) bears beautiful displays of small purple-pink flowers and grows in the mild climates of the southern states and along the Atlantic coast. It grows as an annual in seasonally wet soils. Camphor pluchea (*P. camphorata*) grows in similar coastal habitats in the Southeast.

## USES

**Ornamental**

**Containers**

**Rain garden/wetland/stormwater management**

## ADDITIONAL HOST PLANT FOR:

Rufous geometer moth (*Xanthotype rufaria*), Southern emerald moth (*Synchlora frondaria*)

## NATIVE RANGE

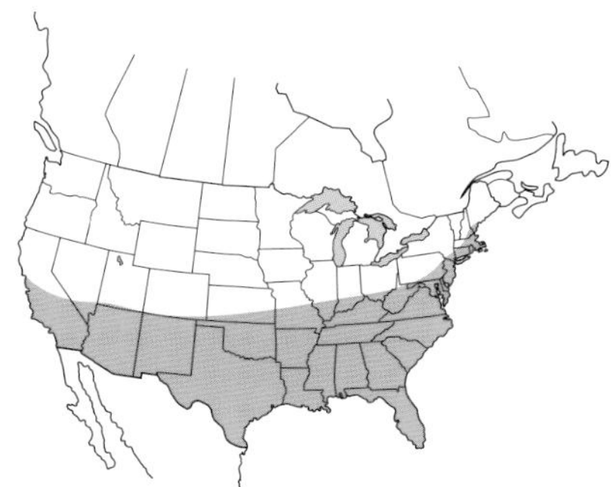

| FLOWER COLOR | HEIGHT | AVAILABILITY |
| --- | --- | --- |
| Purple, pink | 1 to 3 feet (0.3 to 0.9 m) | Variable by region |

75.

ASTERACEAE

# Tickseed

*Coreopsis* spp.

Drawing large numbers of monarchs with abundant nectar may not be its major strength, but coreopsis costs little, is easy to establish, has a long bloom time, and tolerates dry, sandy, tough conditions. Those qualities make these wildflowers—both annual and perennial species—extremely valuable for a wide range of garden and conservation applications.

Some coreopsis species spread by underground rhizomes; most produce multiple showy flower heads on each plant. Xerces has used a number of different species in our own projects and observed excellent results in

| EXPOSURE | SOIL MOISTURE | BLOOM TIME |
|---|---|---|
| Sun | Medium | Summer |

mass plantings along roadsides, in dry and exposed parking strips, as well as in raised beds and plantings around sunny house foundations. Large group plantings of coreopsis will attract the most butterflies, and many members of this genus also mix well with blanketflower and black-eyed Susan, both of which require the same soil conditions.

## RECOMMENDED SPECIES

Approximately two dozen species of coreopsis are found in the United States and Canada, with the greatest diversity in the southeastern states, where several rare and uncommon species have been found.

Large-flowered coreopsis (*C. grandiflora*) extends across the Southeast, especially the lower Mississippi River valley. The compact and reliable lanceleaf coreopsis (*C. lanceolata*) occurs from Minnesota to Texas and east to Florida. Plains coreopsis (*C. tinctoria*), with its striking, often red-and-yellow flowers, is an annual of the Midwest and West, where it can be found reseeding itself in harsh locations such as truck stop parking lots or emerging from pavement cracks in windswept Great Plains roadsides.

---

## USES

**Ornamental**

**Wildflower meadow/prairie restoration**

**Neglected areas/tough sites**

## ADDITIONAL HOST PLANT FOR:

The wavy-lined emerald or camouflaged looper moth (*Synchlora aerata*), which uses pieces of the tickseed flowers or plant and attaches them to its body as camouflage

## NATIVE RANGE

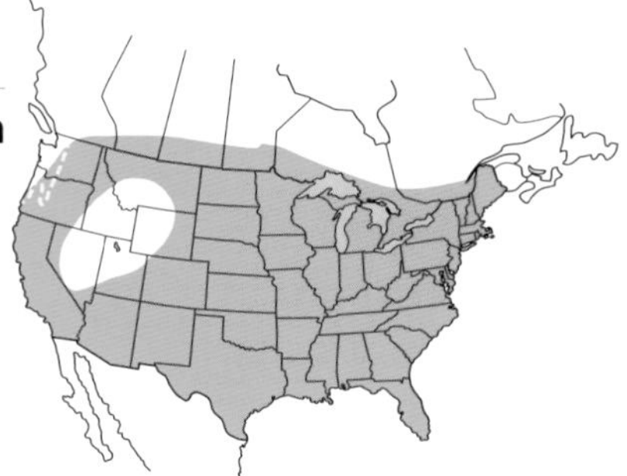

| FLOWER COLOR | HEIGHT | AVAILABILITY |
|---|---|---|
| Yellow, occasionally red or white | 6 feet (1.8 m) | Wide |

76.

VERBENACEAE

# Vervain

*Verbena* spp.

Several dozen native and nonnative vervain species are found in North America, including some weedy species and a few rare habitat specialists. Our native vervains can be less showy than popular nonnative ornamentals but are very well adapted to a wide range of conditions. Locally native species are present in nearly every natural ecosystem in the United States and southern Canada, providing nectar for monarchs.

Unfortunately, most of these species are not available in native plant nurseries. Where available, however, they are mostly trouble-free, interesting

| EXPOSURE | SOIL MOISTURE | BLOOM TIME |
|---|---|---|
| Sun | Wet to dry | Summer |

plants with clusters of flowers that open sequentially, providing long bloom periods and extended nectar for butterflies. Native vervains are also host plants for the common buckeye butterfly (*Junonia coenia*).

## RECOMMENDED SPECIES

The two most commonly commercially available vervain include hoary vervain (*V. stricta*) and blue vervain (*V. hastata*). Hoary vervain occurs mostly in the central United States and southern Ontario and can tolerate slightly drier soils than blue vervain, which is found across most of the northern United States and southern Canada and prefers damp locations. Western vervain (*V. lasiostachys*) provides nectar to monarchs during key periods of their breeding season across the western United States. Xerces is working with native plant nurseries to increase the supply of Western vervain to create quality habitat for Western monarchs.

## USES

**Ornamental**

**Containers**

**Wildflower meadow/prairie restoration**

**Rain garden/wetland**

## ADDITIONAL HOST PLANT FOR:

Fine-lined sallow moth (*Catabena lineolata*), common buckeye butterfly (*Junonia coenia*). Larvae of the verbena bud moth (*Endothenia hebesana*) feed on the developing seeds of vervain.

## NATIVE RANGE

| FLOWER COLOR | HEIGHT | AVAILABILITY |
| --- | --- | --- |
| Blue, white, purple, pink | 1 to 4 feet (0.3 to 1.2 m) | Variable by region |

77.

ASTERACEAE

# Wingstem, Frostweed

*Verbesina* spp.

Although tall and sometimes described as "gangly," wingstem's interesting stem shape (with parallel flanges, or wings, along the stem) and bright flowers are an attractive addition to ornamental shade gardens. Once the flowers have been pollinated and the seeds develop, gently press the seed head open to reveal marvelous **achenes** (dry, one-seed fruits) with a cat's-eye pattern.

| EXPOSURE | SOIL MOISTURE | BLOOM TIME |
| --- | --- | --- |
| Shade to part sun | Wet to average | Summer |

Most species grow best in damp, slightly shaded sites such as drainage ditches, stream banks, moist woodland edges, floodplains, and riparian (river) buffers. In addition to feeding monarch butterflies, wingstem (also called crownbeard or frostweed, depending on the species) attracts extremely large numbers of beneficial insects. The hollow stems provide suitable nesting habitat for leafcutter and mason bees, and the plant is a caterpillar host for the bordered patch butterfly and gold moth.

Various species are widely distributed, and the most common are also the best nectar and pollen plants. Commercial seed sources are limited but slowly increasing in availability.

## RECOMMENDED SPECIES

Look for common wingstem (*V. alternifolia*), golden crownbeard (*V. encelioides*), and white crownbeard (*V. virginica*).

## USES

**Ornamental**

**Wildflower meadow/prairie restoration**

**Hedgerow/screen/shade**

**Rain garden/wetland/stormwater management**

## NATIVE RANGE

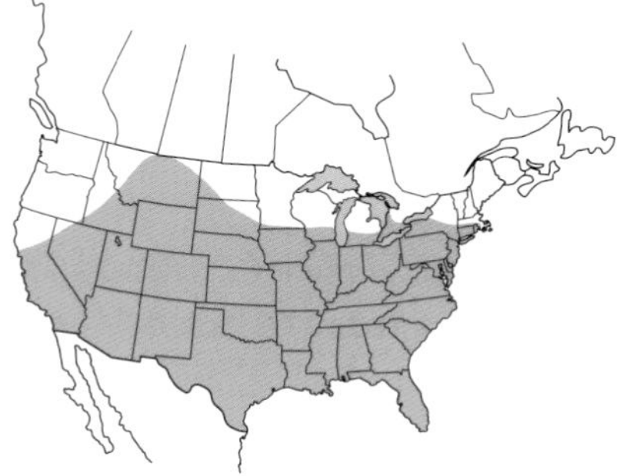

## ADDITIONAL HOST PLANT FOR:

Silvery checkerspot (*Chlosyne nycteis*) and bordered patch butterflies (*Chlosyne lacinia*), and gold moth (*Basilodes pepita*)

| FLOWER COLOR | HEIGHT | AVAILABILITY |
|---|---|---|
| Yellow, white | 8 feet (2.4 m) | Variable by region |

# 78.

LAMIACEAE

# Wood Mint

*Blephilia* spp.

Also known as pagoda-plant, for the stacked clusters of pale purple flowers along its stems, wood mint blooms throughout midsummer. Great for dry, shady yards or flower beds, these species deserve more attention as nectar plants and ornamentals, especially since they thrive and bloom in shady locations.

Characteristic of the mint family, wood mint's rhizomes enable it to spread slowly and expand from its original location. In addition to monarchs, the plant provides nectar to bumblebees and leafcutter bees.

## USES

**Ornamental**

**Hedgerow/screen/shade**

## RECOMMENDED SPECIES

Downy pagoda-plant (*B. ciliata*) and hairy pagoda-plant (*B. hirsuta*)

## NATIVE RANGE

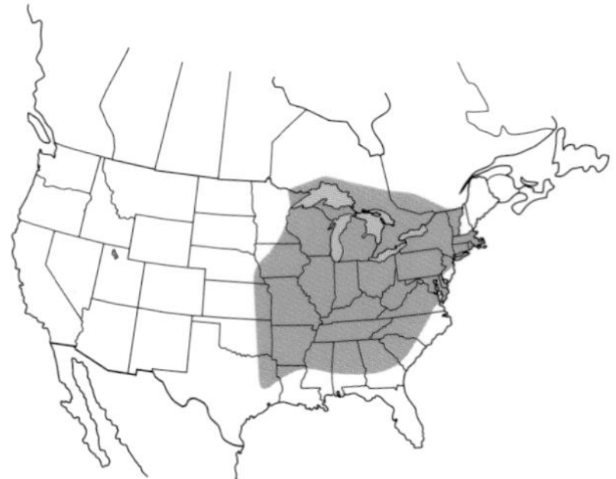

**ADDITIONAL HOST PLANT FOR:** *Blephilia* spp. are excellent for bees, but few other insects are known to feed on these plants.

| EXPOSURE | SOIL MOISTURE | BLOOM TIME |
|---|---|---|
| Part shade to shade | Dry | Late spring and summer |

| FLOWER COLOR | HEIGHT | AVAILABILITY |
|---|---|---|
| White, blue, purple | 2 feet (0.6 m) | Variable by region |

# 6

# Nectar Plants: Trees, Shrubs, and Vines

Not to be overlooked, nectar-producing trees and shrubs can provide extremely important butterfly food resources in some locations. This is especially the case in the arid Southwest and southern California, where the deep root systems of drought-tolerant desert shrubs can support flowers even in some of the hottest seasons.

Conversely, in temperate climates, trees and shrubs are often the first spring-flowering plants to bloom en masse, welcoming early-arriving monarchs with an abundant source of energy weeks before prairie wildflowers begin their midyear peak bloom.

79.

ASTERACEAE

# Baccharis, False Willow

*Baccharis* spp.

Although this sunflower family member is typically characterized by herbaceous wildflowers, *Baccharis* is, surprisingly, a group of woody shrubs. An important nectar source at monarch overwintering sites in California, these white-flowered plants are also some of the latest nectar producers in their respective regions, sometimes blooming in midwinter. This trait has made them popular choices in many of the larger habitat restoration projects Xerces has worked on for monarchs and other pollinators in hot climates and at overwintering sites, where late-season forage may be important.

| EXPOSURE | SOIL MOISTURE | BLOOM TIME |
|---|---|---|
| Sun | Dry to wet | Fall |

Most *Baccharis* species are very tolerant of drought, saline soils, and occasional flooding, making them useful for difficult site conditions. They are also generally deer resistant: their suckering growth habit promotes small, clumping thickets that help plants recover from any physical damage. In nature these tough plants are found near seasonal streams (especially in the Southwest) and saltwater estuaries (along the Atlantic and Gulf coasts).

## RECOMMENDED SPECIES

Twenty-three species of *Baccharis* occur along both the East and West Coasts, as well as across the southern half of the United States. The greatest diversity of species is located in the Southwest, and most are not hardy in cold climates. Note that many *Baccharis* produce separate male and female plants, and while nectar-seeking monarchs may visit both, other flower visitors such as native bees may prefer male (pollen-bearing) plants.

Common species that are typically available from native plant nurseries include sea myrtle (*B. halmifolia*), which occurs from southern New England south along the Atlantic and Gulf coasts to Texas; coyote brush (*B. pilularis*), which is a West Coast native ranging from Oregon to California and available in several cultivated varieties; and two species occurring in the Southwest from Texas to California: mule-fat (*B. salicifolia*) and willow baccharis (*B. salicina*).

## USES

**Hedgerow/screen/shade**

**Rain garden/wetland/stormwater management**

## ADDITIONAL HOST PLANT FOR:

Dozens of moths feed on this diverse genus of plants. Several are borers.

| FLOWER COLOR | HEIGHT | AVAILABILITY |
| --- | --- | --- |
| White | 12 feet (3.7 m) | Wide |

80.

CLEOMACEAE/CAPPARACEAE

# Beeplant, Bladderpod

*Cleome* spp., *Isomeris* spp., *Peritoma* spp.

Lanky but dazzling, this purple-flowered western dryland plant has long been considered an important pollinator plant as well as a great ornamental. Also known as spiderflower, beeplant is a suitable garden or container plant throughout the country. Spiny bracts develop at the base of each leaf; the fruits grow into slender pods that rattle with seeds. Beeplant tolerates soil and climate conditions where few other plants grow, making them regionally important in the arid West as well as useful for neglected areas or tough soils.

| EXPOSURE | SOIL MOISTURE | BLOOM TIME |
|---|---|---|
| Sun | Wet to dry | Summer |

## RECOMMENDED SPECIES

In the deserts of southern California, the shrub bladderpod (*Peritoma arborea*, formerly *Isomeris arborea*) also survives on minimal annual rainfall, while blooming abundantly and almost continuously throughout the year. It is very important as a nectar plant for monarchs at the beginning and end of overwintering, when fewer food sources are available. It is also an excellent choice for farm hedgerows in drought-prone areas.

The related annual wildflower, Rocky Mountain beeplant (*Cleome serrulata*), grows in disturbed semimoist rangeland soils. Its close relative, the annual yellow beeplant (*C. lutea*), grows in even harsher conditions, including areas with alkali soils and less than 10 inches (25 cm) of annual rainfall.

## USES

**Ornamental**

**Containers**

**Wildflower meadow/prairie restoration**

**Neglected areas/tough sites**

**Hedgerow/screen/shade**

**Xeriscape**

## NATIVE RANGE

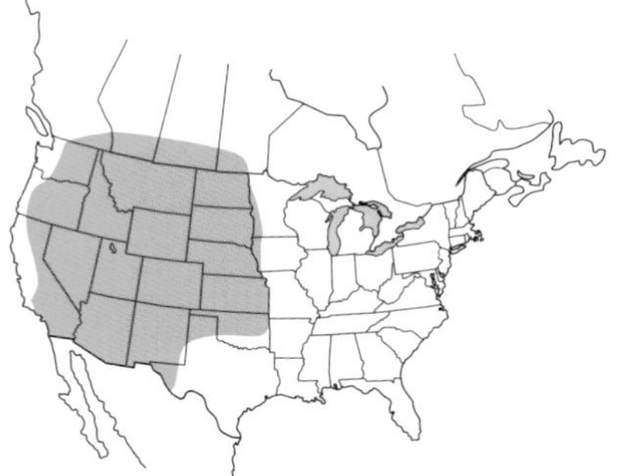

## ADDITIONAL HOST PLANT FOR:

Checkered white (*Pontia protodice*) and Becker's white (*Pontia beckerii*) butterflies

| FLOWER COLOR | HEIGHT | AVAILABILITY |
|---|---|---|
| Purple, pink, yellow, white | 4 feet (1.2 m) | Wide |

# 81. ASTERACEAE Brittlebush

*Encelia* spp.

These members of the sunflower family are all resinous desert plants, many with dusky blue-gray foliage and flowers that resemble those of coreopsis, black-eyed Susan, or blanketflower. The cheery yellow blooms tend to appear after periodic rain events, while the shrubby foliage is the dominant feature during long, dry periods when the plant is not flowering.

Brittlebushes are useful as ground covers for mass planting or as erosion control plants in xeriscape gardens, where their clumping form can both define a space and provide cover for multiple species of small desert

| EXPOSURE | SOIL MOISTURE | BLOOM TIME |
|---|---|---|
| Full sun | Dry | Spring |

animals. For an arid-region plant, brittlebush is considered short-lived, with individual plants reportedly not persisting longer than a few decades. It is also a fire-adapted species, and although it does not always resprout after fires, it does reseed itself across burned lands. Cold is the one climatic feature these desert-adapted plants do not handle well. Many desert gardeners describe them as not very frost tolerant.

## RECOMMENDED SPECIES

Eight species of brittlebush are found in the United States, all limited to the Southwest, from California to Texas. Two of the more widespread and adaptable species include common brittlebush (*E. farinosa*), which occurs across the Southwest, and California brittlebush (*E. californica*), a native of southern California.

## USES

**Ornamental**

**Neglected areas/tough sites**

**Xeriscape**

## ADDITIONAL HOST PLANT FOR:

Dwarf tawny wave moth (*Cyclophora nanaria*), fatal metalmark butterfly (Calephelis nemesis)

## NATIVE RANGE

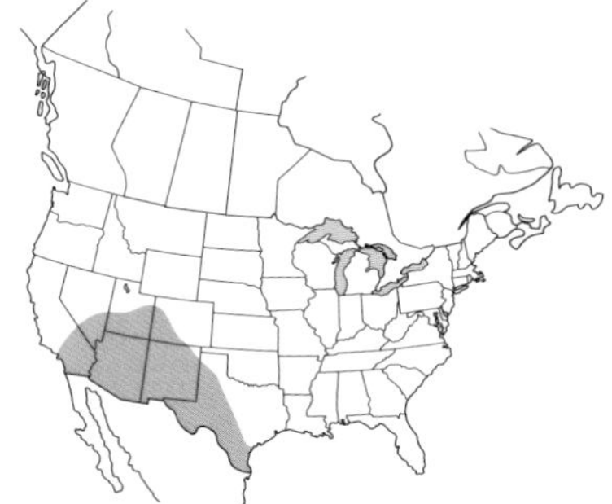

| FLOWER COLOR | HEIGHT | AVAILABILITY |
|---|---|---|
| Yellow | 1 to 4 feet (0.3 to 1.2 m) | Limited; variable by region |

# 82.

RUBIACEAE

# Buttonbush

*Cephalanthus* spp.

Several outstanding features help make buttonbush a notable wetland shrub. Its round fruits, which are clusters of wedge-shaped seeds, hang on the open, twisted branches throughout the fall and winter, creating visual interest. Those fruits develop from puffball groups of small, tubelike flowers—a rich nectar source for monarch butterflies. The attractive foliage makes it equally interesting as an ornamental plant, especially in damp locations.

Buttonbush is one of the few native shrubs that provides midsummer blooms for pollinators and also grows well in wet soils and shade. In restoration

| EXPOSURE | SOIL MOISTURE | BLOOM TIME |
|---|---|---|
| Part shade to shade; tolerates sun where soils are wet | Wet to moist | Summer |

projects, typical applications for buttonbush include wetland revegetation and soil stabilization along streams and drainage areas. In past times, buttonbush was an important honey plant in the lower Mississippi River floodplain.

In addition to monarchs, many other large butterflies, hummingbird moths, and hummingbirds flutter around the blooms.

## RECOMMENDED SPECIES

Common buttonbush (*C. occidentalis*) occurs natively across most of the United States. Although at least one ornamental variety of buttonbush has been developed, it doesn't offer any particular advantages over the wild-type species.

---

## USES

**Ornamental**

**Hedgerow/screen/shade**

**Rain garden/wetland/stormwater management**

## ADDITIONAL HOST PLANT FOR:

Buttonbush is a host plant for caterpillars of some of our largest and showiest moths, including the titan sphinx (*Aellopos titan*), the hydrangea sphinx (*Darapsa versicolor*), and the royal walnut moth (*Citheronia regalis*).

## NATIVE RANGE

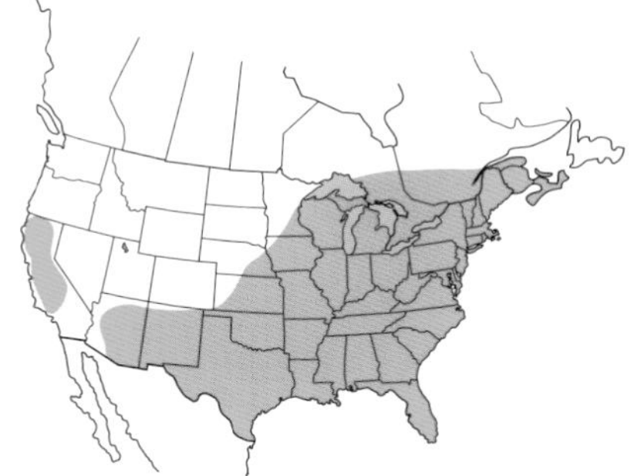

| FLOWER COLOR | HEIGHT | AVAILABILITY |
| --- | --- | --- |
| White, pink | To 12 feet (3.7 m) | Variable by region |

83.

SAPINDACEAE/HIPPOCASTANACEAE

# California Buckeye

*Aesculus californica*

With a native range limited to central and coastal California, this medium-sized hardwood tree has a fairly specific role as a Western monarch plant. Yet within that region it is considered a preeminent nectar producer, with few rivals for the sheer number and diversity of butterflies that it attracts.

Beyond just monarchs, California butterfly watchers have recorded mourning cloaks, red admirals, Lorquin's admirals, California sisters, Northern checkerspots, Edith's checkerspots, California tortoiseshells, West Coast ladies, painted ladies, buckeyes, satyr anglewings, Callippe fritillaries,

| EXPOSURE | SOIL MOISTURE | BLOOM TIME |
|---|---|---|
| Sun to partial shade | Wet to average | Late spring |

California ringlets, large marbles, great coppers, echo blues, Acmon blues, hedgerow hairstreaks, Dryope hairstreaks, great purple hairstreaks, California hairstreaks, umber skippers, mournful duskywings, Propertius duskywings, anise swallowtails, pale swallowtails, Western tiger swallowtails, two-tailed swallowtails, and pipevine swallowtails. In some cases, people have observed up to 200 individual butterflies on a single tree while it is in bloom!

Surprisingly, although California buckeye is renowned as a nectar producer, its nectar is toxic to honey bees. Native insects, including monarchs and bumblebees, do not seem to be affected.

California buckeye is a very long-lived species, with an estimated life span of more than 200 years. These trees are also notable for producing the largest seed of any known temperate plant. They tolerate a range of soil conditions, from damp canyon bottoms to dry exposed hillsides, and comingle excellently with various oaks and *Ceanothus* species.

## RECOMMENDED SPECIES

No known varieties or ornamental selections exist for California buckeye, although five other members of the *Aesculus* genus are found across North America, including the well-known Ohio buckeye (*A. glabra*). Many of these species have large, showy flowers and may be excellent pollinator trees in their respective regions.

## USES

**Ornamental**

**Hedgerow/screen/shade**

## ADDITIONAL HOST PLANT FOR:

Echo azure butterfly (*Celastrina echo*)

## NATIVE RANGE

| FLOWER COLOR | HEIGHT | AVAILABILITY |
|---|---|---|
| White | 30 feet (9 m) | Wide |

# 84.

## RHAMNACEAE

# Ceanothus, New Jersey Tea, Wild Lilac

*Ceanothus* spp.

Native only to North America, *Ceanothus* are some of our showiest and most densely flowered native shrubs. Moreover, many of these 50 to 60 different species can be intensely fragrant when flowering; all are highly attractive to pollinators. These characteristics, combined with their typical form as multistemmed shrubs, make them excellent native alternatives to the widely planted nonnative butterflybush (*Buddleja* spp.), which can become invasive in some regions.

Other notable attributes of these plants include excellent drought tolerance by most species, and nitrogen-fixing root systems that allow them to thrive even in low-fertility soils. Along with nectar-seeking monarchs, many other interesting pollinators flock to *Ceanothus* blossoms, and the foliage is a caterpillar food source for the gorgeous and exceptionally large wild ceanothus silk moth, which is as visually striking as any butterfly.

Wild lilacs are sometimes noted for being relatively short-lived, often dying after 20 or 30 years, although this is by no means true of all species. They are, however, susceptible to heavy deer browsing and may need protection where deer populations are high. Most species are evergreen except for those adapted to cold climates, which lose their leaves in the fall.

| EXPOSURE | SOIL MOISTURE | BLOOM TIME |
|---|---|---|
| Sun | Medium | Spring |

| FLOWER COLOR | HEIGHT | AVAILABILITY |
|---|---|---|
| White, blue, pink | 1 to 12 feet (0.3 to 3.7 m) | Variable by region; wide |

## RECOMMENDED SPECIES

California has the greatest diversity of *Ceanothus*, with various species found only in coastal habitats, mountain foothills, deserts, or serpentine soils. Numerous attractive cultivated varieties and hybrids of these California plants are commercially available, but some believe those nonwild selections have the shortest life spans. Some wild-type plants to seek out from native plant nurseries include buckbrush (*C. cuneatus*), an exceptionally drought-tolerant species that is widespread in California and southern Oregon; New Jersey tea (*C. americanus*), naturally occurring from southeastern Canada to Florida and west into the Great Plains; Fendler's ceanothus (*C. fendleri*), a native of the southern Rocky Mountains; prairie redroot (*C. herbaceus*), found in central North America from Manitoba south to Texas; red stem ceanothus (*C. sanguineus*), a Pacific Northwest native that grows on both sides of the Cascade Mountains; and snowbrush ceanothus (*C. velutinus*), which is distributed across the West and Great Basin from California to Wyoming.

## USES

**Ornamental**

**Hedgerow/screen/shade**

**Xeriscape**

## NATIVE RANGE

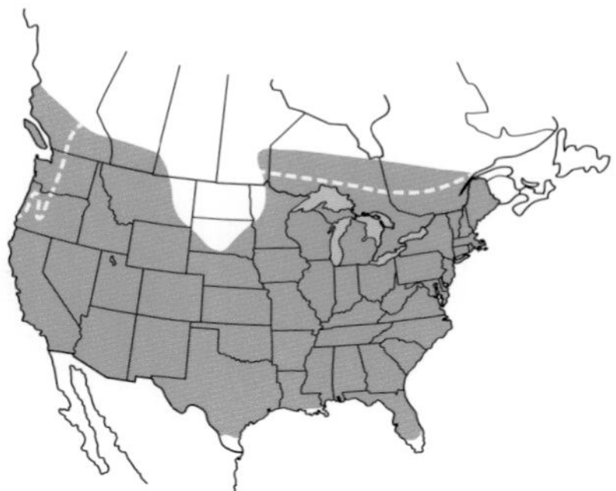

## ADDITIONAL HOST PLANT FOR:

These shrubs are host plants for many dozens of moths and butterflies, including satyrs, summer azure (*Celastrina neglecta*), echo azure (*Celastrina echo*), pale swallowtail (*Papilio eurymedon*), California tortoiseshell (*Nymphalis californica*), ceanothus silkmoth (*Hyalophora euryalus*), and Western sheepmoth (*Hemileuca eglanterina*).

85.

ROSACEAE

# Chokecherry, Wild Cherry, Wild Plum

*Prunus* spp.

In most areas, the various wild cherry and plum species that make up this genus bloom too early to benefit migrating monarchs. In warm climates such as coastal California and Florida, however, where monarchs are present year-round, these can be extremely valuable as one of the first spring nectar resources. In fact, the authors have observed overwintering monarchs in Pacific Grove, California, leave their winter clusters on

| EXPOSURE | SOIL MOISTURE | BLOOM TIME |
|---|---|---|
| Sun to part shade | Medium | Spring |

warm late-winter days to nectar on a nearby *Prunus* species. Occasionally, observers in the Midwest have witnessed fall-migrating monarchs roosting for the night in large black cherry trees, although other deciduous trees are also known to be used for the same purpose.

## RECOMMENDED SPECIES

In warm climates where wild plums and cherries provide early nectar for monarchs, species to look for include bitter cherry (*P. emarginata*) and hollyleaf cherry (*P. ilicifolia*) on the California coast; in Florida, cherry laurel (*P. caroliniana*) and hog plum (*P. umbellata*) are two reliable and widespread species.

## USES

**Ornamental**

**Hedgerow/screen/shade**

## NATIVE RANGE

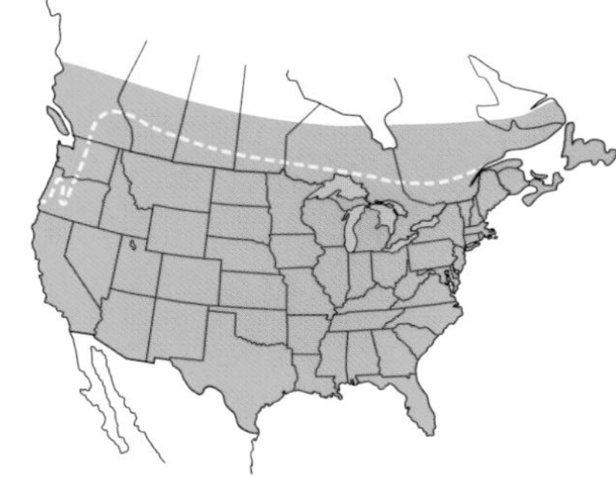

## ADDITIONAL HOST PLANT FOR:

Of all the plant genera in this book, *Prunus* serves as a host plant for the most moth and butterfly species. Several hundred species use *Prunus* as host plants, including the dot-lined white moth (*Artace cribraria*), ultronia underwing moth (*Catocala ultronia*), Western sheepmoth (*Hemileuca eglanterina*), red-spotted purple or white admiral butterfly (*Limenitis arthemis*), Appalachian tiger swallowtail butterfly (*Papilio appalachiensis*), and, infamously, tent caterpillars (*Malacosoma* spp.).

| FLOWER COLOR | HEIGHT | AVAILABILITY |
| --- | --- | --- |
| Pink, white | 6 to 80 feet (1.8 to 24 m) | Variable by region |

# 86.

RANUNCULACEAE

# Clematis, Leather Flower

*Clematis* spp.

Introduced cultivated species and wild native species of clematis are plentiful, totaling nearly 55 in North America. The plants are woody climbing vines with divided leaves and out-of-this-world showy flowers. The seeds have long, fluffy appendages that aid seed dispersal and add visual interest in the fall and winter in the garden or in dried arrangements. Clematis serves as a nectar plant for monarchs and many bee species.

| EXPOSURE | SOIL MOISTURE | BLOOM TIME |
|---|---|---|
| Sun, part shade | Moist to average | Summer |

## RECOMMENDED SPECIES

Monarchs have been reported nectaring on western white clematis (*C. ligusticifolia*) in California. Devil's darning needles (*C. virginiana*), used by monarchs in the East, is easy to cultivate and widely available from native plant nurseries.

## USES

**Ornamental**

**Hedgerow/screen/shade**

## ADDITIONAL HOST PLANT FOR:

Fall clematis clearwing borer moth (*Alcathoe autumnalis*), fatal metalmark (*Calephelis nemesis*)

## NATIVE RANGE

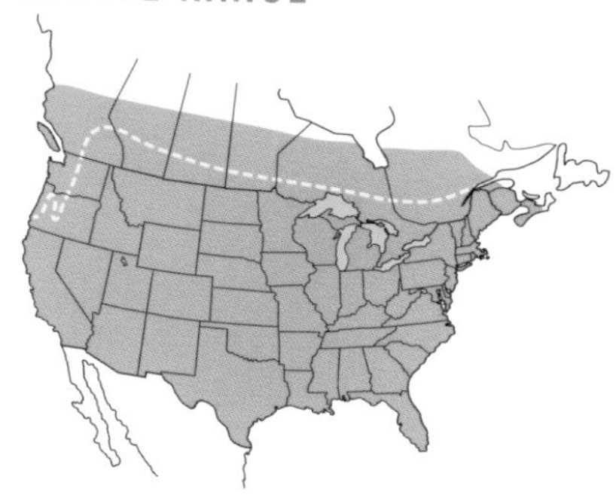

| FLOWER COLOR | HEIGHT | AVAILABILITY |
| --- | --- | --- |
| White, various | Variable with the height of support or trellis | Variable by region |

87.

GROSSULARIACEAE

# Currant, Gooseberry

*Ribes* spp.

Native currants grow across North America. These small shrubs are suited to sites with partial sun; their flowers and stems are valuable for pollinators. The fruits from these species can be made into pies or preserves.

## RECOMMENDED SPECIES

In the West in early spring, golden currant (*R. aureum*) produces an abundance of bright yellow flowers notable for their clove or vanilla fragrance. There are records of monarchs using the flowers for nectar; various

| EXPOSURE | SOIL MOISTURE | BLOOM TIME |
|---|---|---|
| Sun to part shade | Dry to average | Spring |

early-season bees also visit. The plant thrives in dry, exposed locations, spreads by suckering, and is appropriate for revegetation of many sites, as well as for hedgerow use across the inland West.

## USES

**Ornamental**

**Hedgerow/screen/shade**

### ADDITIONAL HOST PLANT FOR:

Gray comma butterfly (*Polygonia progne*), ceanothus silkmoth (*Hyalophora euryalus*), tailed copper butterfly (*Lycaena arota*), hoary comma butterfly (*Polygonia gracilis*), Nuttall's sheepmoth (*Hemileuca nuttalli*), io moth (*Automeris io*), Western sheepmoth (*Hemileuca eglanterina*)

## NATIVE RANGE

| FLOWER COLOR | HEIGHT | AVAILABILITY |
|---|---|---|
| Yellow, green | To 10 feet (3 m) | Wide |

88.

FABACEAE

# False Indigo, Leadplant

*Amorpha* spp.

The combination of delicate compound leaves with a grayish cast (hence the common name leadplant) and purple flower spikes with orange pollen makes false indigo a splashy focal point when it is in full bloom. While this is not a plant that monarchs use very much, large numbers of native bees are active very early in the mornings when the flowers are fresh and offering new pollen. Rise and shine to see a pollinator show!

| EXPOSURE | SOIL MOISTURE | BLOOM TIME |
| --- | --- | --- |
| Sun | Wet to dry | Summer |

## RECOMMENDED SPECIES

The two most common species are leadplant (*A. canescens*), which is a prairie subshrub of drier soils, and the taller false indigo (*A. fruticosa*), which requires moist soils.

## USES

**Ornamental**

**Wildflower meadow/prairie restoration**

**Neglected areas/tough sites**

**Hedgerow/screen/shade**

**Rain garden/wetland/stormwater management**

## NATIVE RANGE

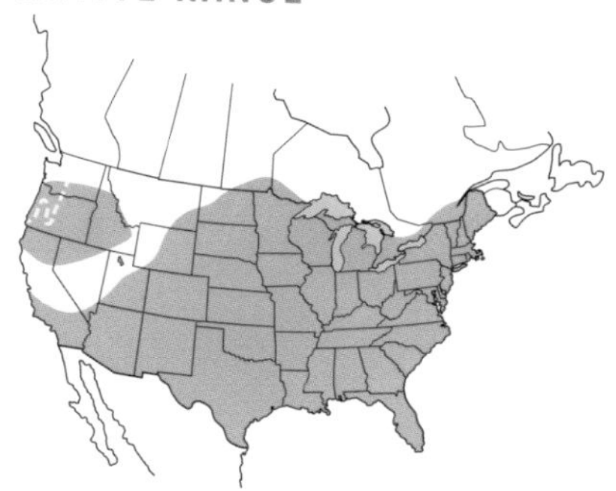

## ADDITIONAL HOST PLANT FOR:

California dogface (*Zerene eurydice*), which is native to California and is recognized as California's state insect and state butterfly; silver-spotted skipper butterfly (*Epargyreus clarus*)

| FLOWER COLOR | HEIGHT | AVAILABILITY |
|---|---|---|
| Purple | To 10 feet (3 m) | Wide |

89.

VERBENACEAE

# Lantana

*Lantana* spp.

A familiar garden and ornamental plant, lantana is native to the tropical and subtropical Americas. In temperate areas it is cultivated as an exotic annual. Although it is an excellent plant for butterflies and popular in gardens for being showy and low maintenance, take care when choosing and planting lantana to avoid introducing invasive species to the surrounding area.

| EXPOSURE | SOIL MOISTURE | BLOOM TIME |
|---|---|---|
| Sun, part shade | Average to dry | Year-round; summer in temperate areas |

## RECOMMENDED SPECIES

For the southern tier of states from California to Florida, West Indian shrubverbena (*L. urticoides*) is a solid choice. Brushland shrubverbena (*L. achyranthifolia*) is native to Arizona, New Mexico, and Texas. Two species native to Florida are depressed shrubverbena (*L. depressa*) and buttonsage (*L. involucrata*), but the spread of garden lantana (*L. camara*) and other factors threaten these native species in the wild. The nonnative trailing shrubverbena (*L. montevidensis*) is an exotic, and garden lantana (*L. camara*) escapes cultivation and naturalizes in southern areas with mild winters.

## USES

**Ornamental**

**Containers**

**Hedgerow/screen/shade**

## ADDITIONAL HOST PLANT FOR:

Lantana stick moth (*Neogalea sunia*), Cross's wave moth (*Leptostales crossii*), lantana plume moth (*Lantanophaga pusillidactyla*)

## NATIVE RANGE

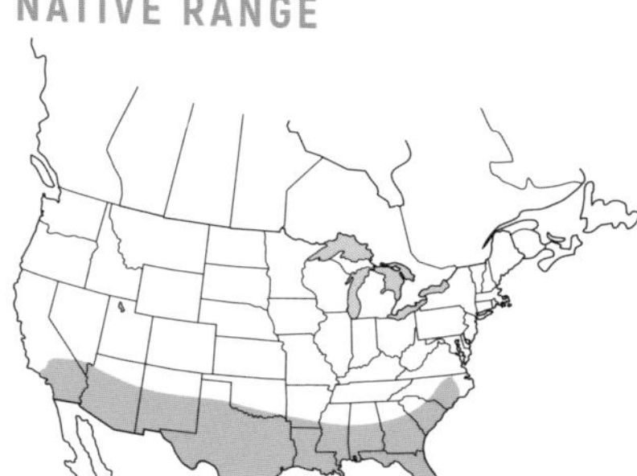

**FLOWER COLOR**

Yellow, orange, various in cultivated varieties

**HEIGHT**

1 to 8 feet (0.3 to 2.4 m)

**AVAILABILITY**

Native species are harder to find than cultivated varieties.

# 90.

ERICACEAE

# Manzanita

*Arctostaphylos* spp.

Related to blueberries, manzanitas make up a huge group of flowering trees and shrubs, with the greatest diversity found in California. Kinnikinnick or bearberry (*A. uva-ursi*), a species found throughout most of the western and northern United States and Canada, is an excellent pollinator plant and a great ground cover. Some manzanitas are said to have so much nectar that it can easily be shaken from flowers on warm days.

| EXPOSURE | SOIL MOISTURE | BLOOM TIME |
|---|---|---|
| Sun | Average | Spring |

## RECOMMENDED SPECIES

Kinnikinnick or bearberry (*A. uva-ursi*) is readily available and suitable for northern and mountain regions. In the West, common or whiteleaf manzanita (*A. manzanita*), greenleaf manzanita (*A. patula*), bigberry manzanita (*A. glauca*), and Pajaro manzanita (*A. pajaroensis*) appear occasionally at specialty native plant nurseries, especially in California.

## USES

**Ornamental**

**Hedgerow/screen/shade**

## ADDITIONAL HOST PLANT FOR:

Ceanothus silkmoth (*Hyalophora euryalus*), Mendocino saturnia moth (*Saturnia mendocino*), splendid royal moth (*Citheronia splendens*), hoary elfin butterfly (*Callophrys polios*), black-banded orange moth (*Epelis truncataria*)

## NATIVE RANGE

| FLOWER COLOR | HEIGHT | AVAILABILITY |
|---|---|---|
| White, pink | 20 feet (6 m) | Wide |

91.

ASTERACEAE

# Rabbitbrush

*Chrysothamnus* spp., *Ericameria* spp.

Resembling tall, woody versions of goldenrod, the various rabbitbrush species are some of the latest-blooming plants across arid sage-steppe western lands and near monarch overwintering sites in California. Their very late bloom (often after the first frost) makes these plants extremely valuable for late-season migrating pollinators, or for bees and butterflies heading into overwintering dormancy. They also are incredibly tough—able to survive fires, occasional animal browsing, saline soils, prolonged drought, blistering sun, extreme cold, and harsh winds.

| EXPOSURE | SOIL MOISTURE | BLOOM TIME |
| --- | --- | --- |
| Full sun | Dry | Summer to fall |

As well as being well-regarded monarch nectar plants, several rabbitbrush species are host plants for the beautiful sagebrush checkerspot butterfly (*Chlosyne acastus*). These small shrubs are not widely available, so ambitious gardeners might consider collecting their own seed from wild populations and starting these hardy, interesting plants as plugs.

Usually found growing with sagebrush, rabbitbrush is common in arid regions of western North America. They are useful rangeland plants, and their abundant blooms add a cheerful late-season splash of yellow color to xeriscape gardens.

## RECOMMENDED SPECIES

Two of the more common, widespread, and hardy species are yellow rabbitbrush (*C. viscidiflorus*) and Greene's rabbitbrush (*C. greenei*); rubber rabbitbrush (*E. nauseosa*) is a showy and excellent late-summer nectar plant when many other sources may be dormant. California goldenbush (*E. ericoides*) blooms from late fall to early winter and occurs naturally as a good nectar source near overwintering sites in California.

## USES

**Ornamental**

**Wildflower meadow/prairie restoration**

**Neglected areas/tough sites**

**Xeriscape**

## NATIVE RANGE

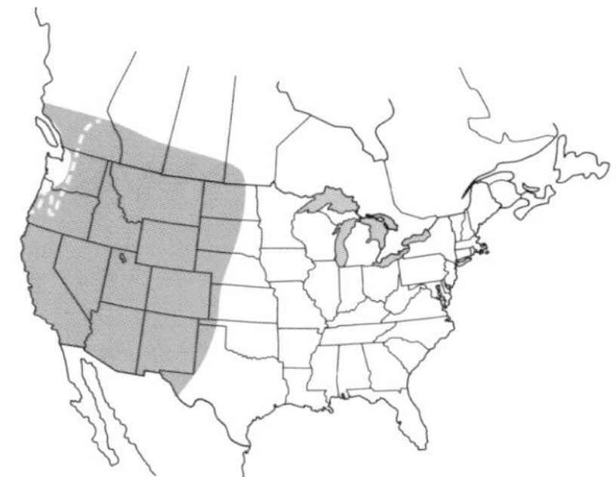

## ADDITIONAL HOST PLANT FOR:

Northern checkerspot butterfly (*Chlosyne palla*), sagebrush checkerspot butterfly (*Chlosyne acastus*)

| FLOWER COLOR | HEIGHT | AVAILABILITY |
|---|---|---|
| Yellow | 1 to 6 feet (0.3 to 1.8 m) | Wide |

92.

ROSACEAE

# Steeplebush, Meadowsweet, Spirea

*Spiraea* spp.

Spiraeas are slender-stemmed shrubs topped with wispy spear-shaped clusters of pink or white flowers. They are in the rose family, and if you look closely you'll see that familiar flower pattern, just at a much tinier scale.

| EXPOSURE | SOIL MOISTURE | BLOOM TIME |
|---|---|---|
| Sun | Wet to average | Midsummer to fall |

Although initially slow growing, once established the plants can hold their own against invasive species such as reed canary grass and Himalayan blackberry. Nearly all spireas integrate wonderfully into home landscaping or hedgerows and complement diverse shrub plantings with long-lasting blooms.

## RECOMMENDED SPECIES

Steeplebush (*S. tomentosa*) and white meadowsweet (*S. alba*) are two widely distributed eastern species with long bloom periods. In the West, Douglas spirea (*S. douglasii*) is widely available from nurseries and establishes easily anywhere with sufficient moisture. In addition to butterflies, spireas attract a wide variety of beneficial insects, especially small flies and wasps and bumblebees.

## USES

**Ornamental**

**Wildflower meadow/prairie restoration**

**Hedgerow/screen/shade**

**Rain garden/wetland/stormwater management**

## NATIVE RANGE

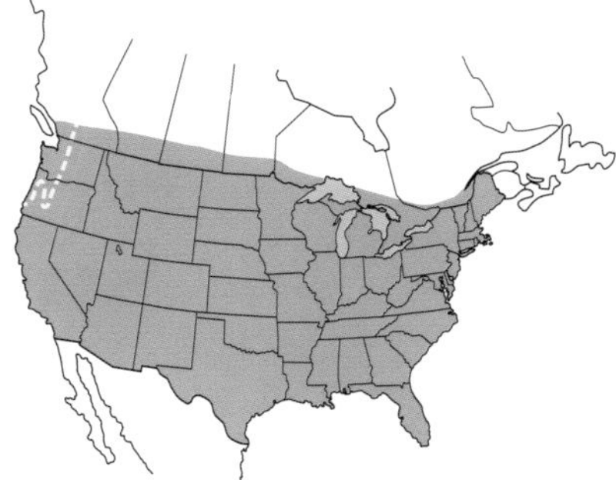

## ADDITIONAL HOST PLANT FOR:

Spring azure butterfly (*Celastrina ladon*)

| FLOWER COLOR | HEIGHT | AVAILABILITY |
|---|---|---|
| White, pink, purple | 4 feet (1.2 m) | Wide |

93.

ANACARDIACEAE

# Sumac

*Rhus* spp.

The clusters of small, shallow flowers on sumac are more often associated with small wild bees, or even ants, than butterflies. Yet there are many recorded observations of monarchs nectaring on the flower spikes of these rhizomatous woody shrubs. Most gardeners are probably familiar with wild sumac in the context of the colonies that tend to grow on forest edges, with few people actually planting these species intentionally. Short-statured creeping varieties do, however, appear occasionally as an interesting and low-maintenance ground cover, favored by landscape architects around

| EXPOSURE | SOIL MOISTURE | BLOOM TIME |
| --- | --- | --- |
| Sun to partial shade | Medium | Summer |

large buildings. Sumacs also provide occasional value for erosion stabilization on slopes and reclamation of mines and abandoned industrial sites.

A few species have growth forms more similar to small trees than shrubs, which can make them interesting specimen plants for sites where larger trees may not fit and smaller plants may not be desirable. In addition to benefiting monarchs and other pollinators, sumac shrubs produce small, dry, vitamin-rich, lemon-tasting berries that songbirds consume throughout fall and winter.

## RECOMMENDED SPECIES

Many species of sumac have very limited commercial availability. Some that may occasionally appear in nurseries include the low-growing and thicket-forming fragrant sumac (*R. aromatica*) and smooth sumac (*R. glabra*), both of which occur naturally across much of the eastern United States and Canada. In the West, skunkbush (*R. trilobata*) is widespread, hardy, and drought resistant, and sometimes available from conservation-oriented nurseries.

## USES

**Neglected areas/tough sites**

**Hedgerow/screen/shade**

## ADDITIONAL HOST PLANT FOR:

Luna moth (*Actias luna*), Neumoegen's buckmoth (*Hemileuca neumoegeni*), red-banded hairstreak butterfly (*Calycopis cecrops*), royal walnut moth (*Citheronia regalis*)

## NATIVE RANGE

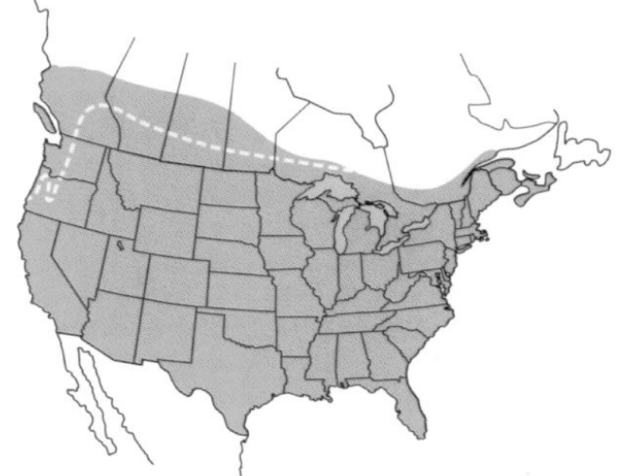

| FLOWER COLOR | HEIGHT | AVAILABILITY |
|---|---|---|
| White, yellow, red | 2 to 20 feet (0.6 to 6 m) | Wide |

94.

ASTERACEAE

# Sweetbush

*Bebbia* spp.

The genus *Bebbia* includes a single species, sweetbush (*B. juncea*). Sweetbush grows from southern California, Nevada, and Arizona into adjacent parts of Utah and New Mexico. This is a perennial shrub in the sunflower family (Asteraceae), reaching up to 5 feet (1.5 m) high.

The flower heads only have florets of the disk type—there are no showy rays or petals in a ring around the outer edge of the head. As the name implies, the flowers are full of sweet nectar, and the plant is an excellent

| EXPOSURE | SOIL MOISTURE | BLOOM TIME |
| --- | --- | --- |
| Sun | Dry | Spring and summer, to year-round |

resource for butterflies and bees. The foliage is also aromatic. Although valuable for nectar, sweetbush flowers are small, so this is not an especially colorful or showy plant, but it's a good choice for dry areas.

## USES

**Neglected areas/tough sites**

**Xeriscape**

## ADDITIONAL HOST PLANT FOR:

Wright's metalmark (*Calephelis wrighti*)

## NATIVE RANGE

| FLOWER COLOR | HEIGHT | AVAILABILITY |
| --- | --- | --- |
| Yellow | To 5 feet (1.5 m) | Limited |

95.

CLETHRACEAE

# Sweetpepperbush

*Clethra* spp.

The fragrant flower spikes of sweetpepperbush typically hum with bumblebees when this distant relative of blueberries and azaleas blooms in summer months across the Northeast and Southeast. Yet they are equally attractive to monarchs and other large butterflies such as various swallowtails. Naturally occurring in wet forests and bogs, this is an excellent specimen for shady and damp yards where it stands out for its showy blossoms that give way in the fall to seed clusters resembling peppercorns.

| EXPOSURE | SOIL MOISTURE | BLOOM TIME |
|---|---|---|
| Partial shade | Medium to wet | Summer |

Easy to care for in the right damp conditions, sweetpepperbush is fairly simple to propagate from cuttings, allowing serious gardeners to propagate more shrubs from just a single plant. With a multistem growth habit, sweetpepperbush tends to form suckers, which can be advantageous where hedgerows or vegetative screens are desirable; they can also be trimmed back into a more confined space.

## RECOMMENDED SPECIES

Coastal sweetpepperbush (*C. alnifolia*) occurs along the Atlantic and Gulf coasts, ranging from New England to Texas. Several cultivated varieties of this plant are occasionally available with slight variation in flower size or color. Mountain sweetpepperbush (*C. acuminata*) is found more inland, with the greatest abundance in the central Appalachian Mountains, although it is most likely adapted to a slightly larger range of conditions across the Southeast; it is also the less available of the two species.

## USES

**Ornamental**

**Hedgerow/screen/shade**

**Rain garden/wetland**

## ADDITIONAL HOST PLANT FOR:

Sweetpepperbush nola moth (*Nola clethrae*), bold-feathered grass moth (*Herpetogramma pertextalis*)

## NATIVE RANGE

| FLOWER COLOR | HEIGHT | AVAILABILITY |
| --- | --- | --- |
| White, pink | 2 to 20 feet (0.6 to 6 m) | Variable by region |

96.

ROSACEAE

# Toyon

*Heteromeles arbutifolia*

Once a major component of California's chaparral ecosystem, toyon has dark green, leathery evergreen leaves rising from multiple stems, and long-lasting red berries that are consumed by birds (and frequently used in holiday wreaths). We include it here because monarch butterflies have been observed to nectar on the delicate white sprays of flowers, and a variety of nectar resources are important to the Western monarch population.

| EXPOSURE | SOIL MOISTURE | BLOOM TIME |
| --- | --- | --- |
| Sun | Dry | Spring to early summer |

Toyon is ideal as a specimen shrub or as a screen when planted as a hedge. Its ornamental qualities and ability to survive drought, below-freezing temperatures, and generally tough sites have made it increasingly common as a landscape plant outside California. The hollylike leaves and berries of toyon are supposedly the namesake for the city of Hollywood—not holly itself.

## RECOMMENDED SPECIES

We don't know of any cultivated varieties of toyon; however, the wild type is an excellent plant in its own right that needs no improvement. Toyon can vary in mature size; some local populations occur as small shrubs while others grow to the size of small trees. When buying at a nursery that sells native plants, ask what their experience is with the mature size and shape of the toyon they sell.

## USES

**Ornamental**

**Neglected areas/tough sites**

**Hedgerow/screen/shade**

**Xeriscape**

## ADDITIONAL HOST PLANT FOR:

No use as a host plant is currently known.

## NATIVE RANGE

| FLOWER COLOR | HEIGHT | AVAILABILITY |
| --- | --- | --- |
| White | 30 feet (9 m) | Variable by region |

# 97.

## POLYGONACEAE

# Wild Buckwheat

*Eriogonum* spp.

Although a few species show up in parts of the rainy Northwest, wild buckwheats are semishrubby, late-blooming plants found mostly in arid western lands. They often co-occur with rabbitbrush. With sugar concentrations reportedly as high as 58 percent in the nectar of some wild buckwheats, these are some of the most effective pollinator magnets in their regions. In many parts of the West, wild buckwheat's dozens of species are considered the best plants for attracting not only monarchs but also a seemingly endless parade of various blue butterflies (lycaenids).

Unlike some desert and arid-region wildflowers, these plants are generally beautiful year-round, many exhibiting dusky blue-gray foliage and small, almost succulent leaves. Ornate, hardy, and drought tolerant, they make excellent bedding plants for rock gardens and locations where irrigated landscapes aren't an option. They are also distantly related to the familiar food plant of the same common name!

### RECOMMENDED SPECIES

Of the 230 or so wild buckwheat species found across the western United States and Canada, many are rare, occurring only in specific valleys, isolated deserts, or distinct microclimates. Of the more common species, we like the yellow-blooming sulphur-flower buckwheat (*E. umbellatum*), found in virtually every western state and arid inland British Columbia. The pink-flowered shrubby Wright's buckwheat (*E. wrightii*) ranges from California to Texas. The puffy-flowered cushion buckwheat (*E. ovalifolium*) is a much more compact little plant that works beautifully in rock gardens, ranging throughout the Great Basin and intermountain West.

| EXPOSURE | SOIL MOISTURE | BLOOM TIME |
|---|---|---|
| Sun | Dry | Summer to fall |

| FLOWER COLOR | HEIGHT | AVAILABILITY |
|---|---|---|
| White, yellow, pink | 1 to 6 feet (0.3 to 1.8 m) | Wide |

## USES

**Ornamental**

**Wildflower meadow/prairie restoration**

**Neglected areas/tough sites**

**Xeriscape**

## NATIVE RANGE

**ADDITIONAL HOST PLANT FOR:** Like monarchs with milkweeds, many of the caterpillars that feed on wild buckwheat are monophagous and can eat only one plant. There are many wild buckwheat species and likewise many species of moths and butterflies that use them as host plants: Electra buckmoth (*Hemileuca electra*) feeds on Eastern Mojave buckwheat (*E. fasciculatum*); lupine blue butterfly (*Plebejus lupini*) on sulfphur-flower buckwheat (*E. umbellatum*) and Eastern Mojave buckwheat (*E. fasciculatum*); and Mojave dotted-blue butterfly (*Euphilotes mojave*) on yellowturbans (*E. pusillum*) and kidneyleaf buckwheat (*E. reniforme*).

Other butterfly species that depend on buckwheats as host plants are Rocky Mountain dotted-blue (*Euphilotes ancilla*), Bernardino dotted-blue (*Euphilotes bernardino*), Pacific dotted-blue (*Euphilotes enoptes*), Western square-dotted blue (*Euphilotes battoides*), Mormon metalmark (*Apodemia mormo*), and Sonoran metalmark (*Apodemia mejicanus*).

98.

ROSACEAE

# Wild Rose

*Rosa* spp.

From short shrubs with a few branches to sprawling thickets, wild native roses come in a variety of sizes and growth habitats. One thing these wild roses have in common is that they have not been bred for layers and layers of petals like ornamental roses. Instead, the wild rose flowers have open “faces,” making the pollen and nectar in the center available and accessible for monarchs and many other pollinators. Rose hips (the red fruits containing the seeds) are a source of food for wildlife and can be used in herbal tea.

| EXPOSURE | SOIL MOISTURE | BLOOM TIME |
| --- | --- | --- |
| Partial sun to sun | Moist to average to dry | Late spring to late summer |

## RECOMMENDED SPECIES

For the eastern and central United States, there are several prairie roses that are relatively low growing (*R. carolina, R. arkansana*). These are widely available and persist in meadow or prairie plantings even with grazing or mowing. For rain gardens or wetter sites, the tall, stately swamp rose (*R. palustris*) blooms in late summer. Woods' rose (*R. woodsii*) is adapted to a range of soil and habitat types in the West.

## USES

**Ornamental**

**Wildflower meadow/prairie restoration**

**Neglected areas/tough sites**

**Hedgerow/screen/shade**

**Rain garden/wetland/stormwater management**

## NATIVE RANGE

## ADDITIONAL HOST PLANT FOR:

Western sheepmoth (*Hemileuca eglanterina*), poecila sphinx moth (*Sphinx poecila*), Columbia silkmoth (*Hyalophora Columbia*)

| FLOWER COLOR | HEIGHT | AVAILABILITY |
|---|---|---|
| Light pink, pink, red | 10 feet (3 m) | Wide |

# 99.

SALICACEAE

## Willow

*Salix* spp.

Often providing the first pollen available in late winter and early spring, willows are an important spring food source for bees. The flowers are not showy—just green or white bristles, often with male and female flowers on separate plants. Only male plants provide pollen, but both male and female flowers offer nectar, and monarch butterflies feed on it.

Willows are easily propagated by cuttings and can be coppiced (cut back to stumps) to create dense thickets. Horticultural hybrids, including most weeping willows, are of little value as sources of pollen or nectar;

| EXPOSURE | SOIL MOISTURE | BLOOM TIME |
|---|---|---|
| Sun to shade | Wet to average | Late winter, early spring |

pussy willows are among the better species for pollinators. In California and the southern United States, willow flowers are critical food sources for adult monarchs after the overwintering period. Willows are small to large trees and can be used in borders, large areas with moist soil, or areas that need protection from soil erosion.

## RECOMMENDED SPECIES

Arroyo willow (*S. lasiolepis*) is especially important for monarchs near their overwintering grounds along the California coast and inland in the Northwest and Great Basin—the trees provide nectar during the critical time in early spring when adult monarchs begin feeding again. In the East, willows generally bloom well before monarch butterflies have made their way north. Pussy willow (*S. discolor*) flowers, however, are still important food for native pollinators, and the leaves feed the caterpillars of many other butterfly species, such as Western tiger swallowtail, mourning cloak, Lorquin's and Weidemeyer's admirals, viceroy, red-spotted purple, and various species of hairstreaks, skippers, and sphinx moths. It is also important for specialist mining bees (*Andrena*).

## USES

**Neglected areas/tough sites**

**Hedgerow/screen/shade**

**Rain garden/wetland/stormwater management**

## ADDITIONAL HOST PLANT FOR:

Ceanothus silkmoth (*Hyalophora euryalus*), io moth (*Automeris io*), Western sheepmoth (*Hemileuca eglanterina*), red-spotted purple or white admiral butterfly (*Limenitis arthemis*)

## NATIVE RANGE

| FLOWER COLOR | HEIGHT | AVAILABILITY |
|---|---|---|
| White, yellow, green | 140 feet (43 m) (*S. nigra*) | Wide |

# 100.

HYDROPHYLLACEAE

## Yerba Santa

*Eriodictyon* spp.

Like other natives of the California chaparral, yerba santa thrives in recently burned areas and quickly regrows in shrubby clonal colonies, resprouting from extensive rhizomes. Monarch butterflies and other pollinators, including hummingbirds, flock to the flowers. Despite its magnificent pollinator value, these oily plants are unlikely to win praise from gardeners for their unpleasant smell and sticky, resin-covered leaves and stems.

| EXPOSURE | SOIL MOISTURE | BLOOM TIME |
|---|---|---|
| Sun | Dry | Spring |

Yerba santa is an important nectar plant for monarchs, however. It is also a larval host plant for the large and showy pale swallowtail butterfly (*Papilio eurymedon*). Most species are limited to California and may be available only from specialty native plant nurseries. Look for narrowleaf yerba santa (*E. angustifolium*) and the showier California yerba santa (*E. californicum*).

## USES

**Neglected areas/tough sites**

**Hedgerow/screen/shade**

**Xeriscape**

## ADDITIONAL HOST PLANT FOR:

*Ethmia arctostaphylella* moth; pale swallowtail butterfly (*Papilio eurymedon*)

## NATIVE RANGE

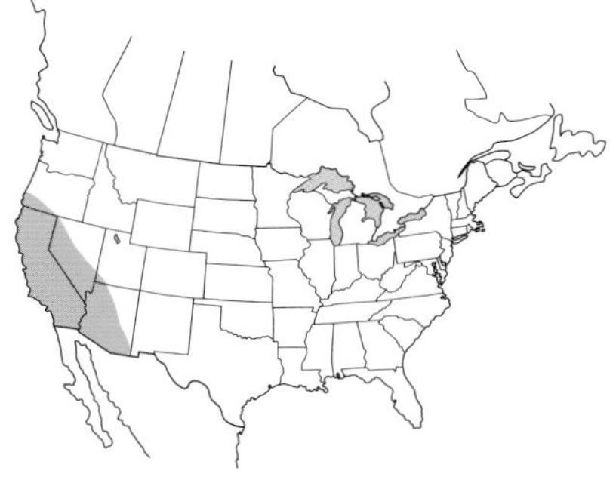

| FLOWER COLOR | HEIGHT | AVAILABILITY |
|---|---|---|
| Purple, white | 8 feet (2.4 m) | Variable by region |

# Appendixes

## Community Science Projects

### Journey North

**https://journeynorth.org/monarchs**

Using community science observations of each monarch life stage and migration, plus the emergence of milkweeds, Journey North tracks this information on maps for the spring and fall seasons.

### Monarch Larva Monitoring Project

**https://monarchjointventure.org/mlmp**

In this community science project led by Monarch Joint Venture, volunteers follow guided activities to collect and submit data on monarch habitat, milkweeds, and the number and survival of caterpillars, as well as tachinid flies, which parasitize monarchs, and aphids, which can alter milkweed quality for monarch use. Monarch Joint Venture has an extensive list of other regional community science opportunities.

### Monarch Watch

**https://www.monarchwatch.org**

Monarch Watch coordinates a tagging program to put numbered stickers on adult monarchs in the eastern United States and to collect data on where those monarchs are tagged and later recovered. They also offer resources for school groups and monarch waystation habitat projects.

### Project Monarch Health

**https://www.monarchparasites.org**

Project Monarch Health studies OE (*Ophryocystis elektroscirrha*), a protozoan parasite of monarchs and closely related species, through the work of volunteers who collect samples from wild butterflies and submit them to the project.

### Western Monarch Milkweed Mapper (WMMM)

**https://www.monarchmilkweedmapper.org**

The WMMM is a community science project of the Xerces Society and partners with the aim to map and better understand monarch butterflies and their milkweed host plants across the western United States. The observations that users submit are used to improve knowledge about where monarchs are, what times of year they are there, which milkweeds and which nectar plants they feed on, and where they are breeding.

Anyone can participate in WMMM by making observations of monarchs, milkweeds, or nectar plants west of the Rocky Mountains. Along with the date and location, take a photo of the observation you are reporting. Create an account on the WMMM website and then upload your photos of monarchs and milkweeds.

Once you have an account, go out and start looking. Check your local parks, natural areas, gardens, and even roadsides. All lifecycle stages of monarchs are of interest, so be sure to check milkweed leaves and stems for caterpillars or eggs. Snap a few photos and then sign in and submit your data via the Milkweed and Monarch Sightings forms.

The WMMM site also offers excellent resources for identifying over 40 milkweed species, as well as other nectar plants, found in the West. Explore the map to see real observations of milkweeds and monarchs and learn what to look for in your area.

### Western Monarch Thanksgiving Count

**https://www.westernmonarchcount.org**

Coordinated by the Xerces Society, the Western Monarch Thanksgiving Count is an annual effort of volunteers to collect data on the status of monarch populations along the California coast during the overwintering season, which occurs from approximately October through February. The majority of this volunteer effort occurs during the Thanksgiving Count (which runs for three weeks surrounding the Thanksgiving holiday) and the New Year's Count (which runs for two weeks starting the weekend before New Year's). Thanks to the extraordinary effort of a cadre of volunteers, the Xerces Society now has over 20 years of data demonstrating that monarchs have undergone a dramatic population decline and a better understanding of the state of their overwintering habitat.

# Resources for Sourcing and Working with the Plants in This Book

## FROM THE XERCES SOCIETY

### Milkweed Seed Finder

**https://xerces.org/milkweed-seed-finder**

Milkweed Seed Finder is an online tool to help gardeners find sources of milkweed plants or seeds. Using pull-down menus and maps, you can search by milkweed species, state, and whether you are looking for plants or seeds. Over 100 active vendors across the country are listed, and the site contains additional resources about milkweeds.

### *Milkweeds: A Conservation Practitioner's Guide*

**https://xerces.org/publications/guidelines/milkweeds-conservation-practitioners-guide**

If you would like to grow your own milkweed seeds or collect responsibly from existing stands, *Milkweeds: A Conservation Practitioner's Guide* is full of information for all areas of the United States.

### Xerces Native Plant Nursery and Seed Directory

**https://xerces.org/pollinator-conservation/native-plant-nursery-and-seed-directory**

Xerces Native Plant Nursery and Seed Directory catalogs over 700 active companies producing and selling native seed and plants and can be filtered by location.

### *Collecting and Using Your Own Wildflower Seed*

**https://xerces.org/publications/guidelines/collecting-and-using-your-own-wildflower-seed**

### *Native Milkweed in California: Planting and Establishment*

https://xerces.org/publications/fact-sheets/native-milkweed-in-california-planting-and-establishment

### Project Milkweed

https://xerces.org/milkweed

## ADDITIONAL RESOURCES

### Native Plant Societies

http://nanps.org/native-plant-societies

# Selected References

**The following are the primary sources of information and data used for this book.**

Agrawal, Anurag. *Monarchs and Milkweed A Migrating Butterfly, a Poisonous Plant, and Their Remarkable Story of Coevolution*. Princeton University Press, 2017.

Borders, Brianna, and Eric Lee-Mäder. *Milkweeds: A Conservation Practitioner's Guide, Plant Ecology, Seed Production Methods, and Habitat Restoration Opportunities*. The Xerces Society for Invertebrate Conservation, 2014.

California Native Plant Society. "Calscape." Accessed September 25, 2019. https://calscape.org/

Canadensys. "Explorer." Accessed October 18, 2019. http://data.canadensys.net/explorer

Consortium of California Herbaria. "CCH2 Portal." Accessed September 25, 2019. https://www.cch2.org/portal/index.php

Kartesz, John T., The Biota of North America Program (BONAP). Taxonomic Data Center. (http://www.bonap.net/tdc). Chapel Hill, N.C. [maps generated from Kartesz, J.T. 2015. Floristic Synthesis of North America, Version 1.0. Biota of North America Program (BONAP). (in press)]. Accessed September 25, 2019. http://bonap.net/napa

Lady Bird Johnson Wildflower Center. "Native Plants Database." Accessed September 25, 2019. https://www.wildflower.org/plants/

Lotts, Kelly, and Thomas Naberhaus, coordinators. "Butterflies and Moths of North America." Accessed September 25, 2019. http://www.butterfliesandmoths.org/

Mader, Eric, Matthew Shepherd, Mace Vaughan, Scott Hoffman Black, and Gretchen LeBuhn. *Attracting Native Pollinators: The Xerces Society Guide, Protecting North America's Bees and Butterflies*. Storey Publishing, 2011.

Matthews, Deborah L., Charles V. Covell, Jr., Katrina M. Lane, and Jacqueline Y. Miller. "Larval Hostplants of Geometridae (Lepidoptera) Collected by Dale H. Habeck in Florida." *Proceedings of the Entomological Society of Washington* 116, no. 1 (2014): 36-68. http://dx.doi.org/10.4289/0013-8797.116.1.36

Robinson, G. S., P. R. Ackery, I. J. Kitching, G. W. Beccaloni, and L. M. Hernández. Natural History Museum, London. "HOSTS—A Database of the World's Lepidopteran Hostplants." Accessed September 25, 2019. http://www.nhm.ac.uk/hosts

Skinner, Mark W., Gretchen LeBuhn, David Inouye, Terry Griswold, and Jennifer Hopwood. United States Department of Agriculture and US Federal Highway Administration "National Database for Pollinator-Friendly Revegetation and Restoration." Accessed September 25, 2019. http://www.nativerevegetation.org/era/

Tallamy, Doug. *Bringing Nature Home: How You Can Sustain Wildlife with Native Plants*. Timber Press, 2009.

United States Department of Agriculture, Natural Resources Conservation Service. "The PLANTS Database." Accessed September 25, 2019. http://plants.usda.gov

University of Alberta Museums, University of Alberta E. H. Strickland Entomological Museum (UASM). "Species dataset." Accessed September 25 2019. https://www.ualberta.ca/museums/museum-collections/eh-strickland-entomological-museum.html

White, Abigail, Jeremie B. Fant, Kayri Havens, Mark Skinner, and Andrea T. Kramer. "Restoring Species Diversity: Assessing Capacity in the United States Native Plant Industry." *Restoration Ecology* 26 (2018): 605-611. https://doi.org/10.1111/rec.12705

Wilhelm, Gerould, and Laura Rericha. *Flora of the Chicago Region*. Indiana Academy of Science, 2017.

Woodson, Jr., Robert E. "The North American Species of *Asclepias* L." *Annals of the Missouri Botanical Garden* 41, no. 1 (1954): 1-211. http://doi.org/10.2307/2394652

The Xerces Society for Invertebrate Conservation. "Monarch Nectar Plant Database." Accessed September 25, 2019. Unpublished dataset.

## Acknowledgments

The authors would like to recognize and thank our fellow Xerces staff for contributing their knowledge, photos, and data to this book: Deedee Soto, Kaitlin Haase, Ray Moranz, Kelly Gill, Sarah Foltz-Jordan, Kitty Bolte, Cameron Newell, Jennifer Hopwood, Mace Vaughan, Karin Jokela, Emma Pelton, Eric Venturini, Brianna Borders, and Stephanie McKnight.

INTERIOR PHOTOGRAPHY BY © Adam Schneider/Alamy Stock Photo, 150; © agatchen/iStock.com, 176; © agefotostock, 1 (l. 2nd fr. b.); © agenturfotografin/stock.adobe.com, 1 (r. 2nd fr. b.); © All Canada Photos/Alamy Stock Photo, 131; © Allison Cherry/iStock.com, 14 c.; © Andrei Stanescu/iStock.com, 144, 282; © Andrew Greaves/Alamy Stock Photo, 1 (b.l.); © Andrew Kearton/Alamy Stock Photo, 160; © ANGHI/iStock.com, 1 (t. 2nd fr. l.); © Annie Otzen/Getty Images, 10; © ArtyAlison/iStock.com, 242; © Aubrey Huggins/Alamy Stock Photo, 50 l.; © Avalong/Photshot License/Alamy Stock Photo, 189; © Axel Gutjahr/stock.adobe.com, 180; © AY Images/Alamy Stock Photo, 157; © badboydt7/iStock.com, 194; © Bill Brooks/Alamy Stock Photo, 29 c., 92, 209 b.; © blickwinkel/Alamy Stock Photo, 230; © bpperry/iStock.com, 1 (l.m.); © Bryan Reynolds/Alamy Stock Photo, 76, 113; © caitlin_w/Getty Images, 16; © CA Wadley/Alamy Stock Photo, 119; © Christina Rollo/Alamy Stock Photo, 1 (t. 2nd fr. r.), 136; © Christopher Price/Alamy Stock Photo, 86; © Chushkin/iStock.com, 255; © Clint Farlinger/Alamy Stock Photo, 25 l., 67; © crbellette/iStock.com, 240; © cturtletrax/iStock.com, 88; © Danita Delimont/Alamy Stock Photo, 159; © Daybreak Imagery/Alamy Stock Photo, 14 l.; © Delbars/iStock.com, 4; © Design Pics Inc/Alamy Stock Photo, 17; Doug Goldman, hosted by the USDA-NRCS PLANTS Database, 103; © epantha/iStock.com, 187; © Erin Bergman/Shutterstock.com, 247; © fgsmiles/stock.adobe.com, 1 (l. 2nd fr. t.), 174; © Florapix/Alamy Stock Photo, 1 (b.c.r.), 216; © Frank Hecker/Alamy Stock Photo, 257; G.A. Cooper, courtesy of Smithsonian Institution, 1 (b. r.); © George Grall/Getty Images, 15 b.; © GeoStills/Alamy Stock Photo, 209 t.; © Gerry Bishop/Alamy Stock Photo, 91; © hanbr/iStock.com, 234; © Hanna Tor/Alamy Stock Photo, 1 (r. 3rd fr. b.); © Heather Spears/Shutterstock.com, 1 (l. 3rd fr. b.), 73; © helga_sm/stock.adobe.com, 60; © Holly Bickerton/Alamy Stock Photo, 65; © ivandzyuba/iStock.com, 140; © James Mundy, Nature's Ark Photography/Alamy Stock Photo, 30, 50 c. & r., 75, 77, 93–96; © Jared Quentin/iStock.com, 268; © Jared Quentin/stock.adobe.com, 70, 71; © jay_a/stock.adobe.com, 214; © jbphotographylt/stock.adobe.com, 168; © Jennifer Tepp/Alamy Stock Photo, 223; © Jerry/stock.adobe.com, 1 (r. 3rd fr. t.), 178; © JHVEPhoto/Alamy Stock Photo, 8, 20 l.; Jim Morefield from Nevada, USA/CC BY-SA 2.0/Wikimedia Commons, 269; © John Richmond/Alamy Stock Photo, 244, 270; © John Serrao/Science Source, 89; © John Skinner, 87; © John Sullivan/Alamy Stock Photo, 1 (r. 2nd fr. t.), 204; © John Van Decker/Alamy Stock Photo, 25 r.; Jomegat/CC BY-SA 3.0/Wikimedia Commons, 29 l.; © Kaleb/stock.adobe.com, 110; © kathyclark777/iStock.com, 225; © Katrin Ray Shumakov/Getty Images, 147; © kazakovmaksim/stock.adobe.com, 218; © Keir Morse, 213; © Ken Barber/Alamy Stock Photo, 260; © Ken Kistler/Alamy Stock Photo, 277; © Kevin Knight/Alamy Stock Photo, 74, 127, 224; © Kevin Schafer/Alamy Stock Photo, 81; © Kristina Blokhin/stock.adobe.com, 279; © Krystyna Szulecka/Alamy Stock Photo, 1 (t.r.); Kusurija/CC BY 3.0/Wikimedia Commons, 29 r.; © Kyle Selcer/Alamy Stock Photo, 1 (r. 4th fr. b.); © LALIT MOHAN SETHEE/iStock.com, 182; © Laurens/stock.adobe.com, 212; © leekris/iStock.com, 21 (3rd fr. t.), 183; © Leena Robinson/Alamy Stock Photo, 13, 21 b.; © LesyaD/iStock.com, 1 (l. 4th fr. b.), 201; © Liliboas/iStock.com, 21 t.; Courtesy of Linda Leinen, 56; © LindaJohnsonbaugh/iStock.com, 35 l.; Mack Hitch, 1 (t.c.l.), 101, 193, 278; © Mantonature/iStock.com, 254; © Maresa Pryor/Danita Delimont/stock.adobe.com, 1 (r. m.), 97; © MariaBrzostowska/iStock.com, 266; © Martin Hughes-Jones/Alamy Stock Photo, 1 (l. 3rd fr. t.); © Martin Ruegner/Getty Images, 6; © mashimara/iStock.com, 1 (t.c.); © Maxal Tamor/Alamy Stock Photo, 68; © MediaMarketing/stock.adobe.com, 46, 61; © Megan McCarty/Alamy Stock Photo, 133; © merrimonc/stock.adobe.com, 104; © Mezmic/iStock.com, 156; © Michael Clay Smith/iStock.com, 184; © Michael G McKinne/Shutterstock.com, 200; © Michel Foret/Alamy Stock Photo, 116; © M. Schuppich/stock.adobe.com, 280; © na9179126124/stock.adobe.com, 250; © Nadezhda_Nesterova/iStock.com, 1 (b.c.l.); © Natural History Collection/Alamy Stock Photo, 158; © Nature and Science/Alamy Stock Photo, 170; © Nick Kurzenko/Alamy Stock Photo, 69; © NNehring/iStock.com, 1 (b.c. & r. 4th fr. t.), 145, 264, 275; © Olga Ionina/stock.adobe.com, 198; © Panther Media GmbH/Alamy Stock Photo, 1 (b. 2nd fr. r.), 84; © Patty Hankins, 192; © PFMphotostock/iStock.com, 256; © pimmimemom/stock.adobe.com, 259; © Prairie Moon Nursery, 151, 202, 207, 233, 249, 253; Courtesy of Prayan Pokharel, 14 r.; © Ray Moranz, 37, 52, 57, 78, 79, 82, 107, 139, 190; © Richard McMillin/iStock.com, 108; © Richard Spellenberg, 59, 62, 99 b.; © Rick & Nra Bowers/Alamy Stock Photo, 173; © Rolf Nussbaumer Photography/Alamy Stock Photo, 258; © Ron Niebrugge/Alamy Stock Photo, 166; © Rose-Marie Murray/Alamy Stock Photo, 221; © Sari O'Neal/Alamy Stock Photo, 21 (2nd fr. t.); © sbonk/iStock.com, 1 (b. 2nd fr. l.); © shapencolour/Alamy Stock Photo, 238; © Skip Moody/Dembinsky Photo Associates/Alamy/Alamy Stock Photo, 15 t., 181; © skymoon13/iStock.com, 134; © Somkak Sarykunthot/Dreamstime.com, 1 (t.l.); © Stan/stock.adobe.com, 142; © Steffen Hauser/botanikfoto/Alamy Stock Photo, 163, 165; © Studio One-One/Getty Images, 35 r.; © Sue Smith/Alamy Stock Photo, 172; © Sundry Photography/Alamy Stock Photo, 272; © Sundry Photography/stock.adobe.com, 210, 252, 261; © tacojim/iStock.com, 196; © Tamara Harding/stock.adobe.com, 109; © T. Iretskaya/iStock.com, 128; © Todd Bannor/Alamy Stock Photo, 149; © Unknown/Alamy Stock Photo, 124; © Universal Images Group North America LLC/Alamy Stock Photo, 55; © watcher fox/Shutterstock.com, 226; © WILDLIFE GmbH/Alamy Stock Photo, 186; © William Eugene Dummitt/Shutterstock.com, 188; © William Tait/Alamy Stock Photo, 154; © Willowpix/iStock.com, 169; © Xerces Society, 1 (l. 4th fr. t.), 36, 51, 53, 63, 83, 98, 99 t., 105, 114, 115, 117, 120, 122, 152, 161, 236, 262; © Zigmunds Kluss/stock.adobe.com, 228; © Zoonar GmbH/Alamy Stock Photo, 1 (t.c.r.), 20 r., 135, 138